BE
MORE
DOG

TRAIN YOUR MIND
TRAIN YOUR DOG

FENELLA NICHOLAS

Matador
9 Priory Business Park,
Wistow Road, Kibworth Beauchamp,
Leicestershire. LE8 0RX
Tel: 0116 279 2299
Email: books@troubador.co.uk
Web: www.troubador.co.uk/matador
Twitter: @matadorbooks

ISBN 978 1838594 893

British Library Cataloguing in Publication Data.
A catalogue record for this book is available from the British Library.

Printed on FSC accredited paper
Printed and bound in Great Britain by 4edge Limited
Typeset in 11pt Minion Pro by Troubador Publishing Ltd, Leicester, UK

Matador is an imprint of Troubador Publishing Ltd

In memory of Willa:
my ever-patient teacher and friend

CONTENTS

"Everyone thinks they have the best dog. And none of them are wrong."

W.R. PURCHE

INTRODUCTION

I am a canine psychologist. Without my pretentious hat on, I'm a dog behaviourist.

Dog behaviourists are not dog trainers. (Although we can do that too.) Training is for human benefit. *Rehabilitation,* which is what I do, is for the dog's benefit. We are primarily people trainers. We help the owners practise a new way of being, which has a direct positive impact on their dogs. Because we are trained in how a dog thinks, we can enlighten the owner and 'fix' any unwanted habits. My job is to change people's perceptions of their dogs, through a better understanding of them, by allowing their pets to be the dogs mother nature intended them to be, before we humans got in the way. Rather unglamorously, I am the creator of normal. If I can return a dog to its normal state, I have done my job and I am happy. We are often called upon as a last resort, when the owner has tried various training methods which have not worked, and the dog is at a threat of being re-homed or put down.

I was recently called to deal with a young male chihuahua who had been growling and baring teeth every time its owner approached with her new baby in her arms. Any passerby on the street who took it upon themselves to bend down and stroke the 'cute' little thing, would get the same snarly treatment. The dog had nipped the mother-in-law, and visitors to the house were met with incessant barking, including me. The couple were at the end of their tether, fearing it was only a matter of time before the dog bit one of their friends, or worse still, their baby. They sent the dog away to live with the wife's mother, who also was not coping, so now they were willing to give it one last try to see if they could take him back.

It became apparent very quickly that Rivington, as he was called, was the boss of the house. This smallest of all dogs held a very elevated position in the household, in the absence of any leadership. It was not the dog's fault that he had become nervous aggressive. He didn't know what decisions to make, but he had to make them, as no one else was picking up the reins. No-one told him to stop barking when a stranger walked in his house, therefore he assumed that this was what was wanted of him, and he learnt to carry on barking, as this stranger was obviously a threat. No-one had told him otherwise. He was unsure of everyone, so he had learnt to keep the threat away by barking and snapping. That seemed to work.

Imagine if you are eight inches tall, and strangers took it upon themselves to loom over you and put a hand towards your head, uninvited. You would probably flinch at first, and if this didn't keep the hands away, you would escalate to a growl. If that warning was ignored you would probably bite. In the long run you would move straight to the bite, as you knew the other stuff didn't work. Rivington did not know he was cute, could not work out why he was attracting so much attention. He did not want the attention. His owners were not doing anything to keep the attention away from him, so he reacted in the only way he knew how.

Once you can see things from a dog's perspective, the picture begins to get a little clearer. This dog was out of balance. Without realising it, and without meaning to, his owners had created his problems by not allowing him to be what he was supposed to be. All dog owners should give their dogs an opportunity to reach their natural potential – doglike, not humanlike. This is a respectful commitment and will create the foundations to bring you and your dog even closer. In the wild, there are no strange behaviours. Obsessions do not exist in a dog's natural habitat. **We** have created them all.

The correct formula for meeting any dog for the first time is 'No touch, no talk, no eye contact.' This is what dogs themselves do. You must first allow the dog to come to you, in his own time, and politely sniff you. This is respectful, and will gain the dog's trust. (A dog will remember you, and other dogs, by smell. The initial sniff is like a handshake and a quick chat, and tells the dog what you ate for lunch, who you live with, or if you are sick.) A high pitched "ooh isn't he adorable!" greeting will heighten the excitement and elicit barking, jumping up, and maybe even a bite, for in the dog's eyes you are unstable. We humans get a great deal of satisfaction from sharing our affection, but while it may be fulfilling our needs, we are not doing the dog any favours.

I taught Rivington's owners some leadership techniques – more on these later – and advised they tell all visitors to the house to ignore him. If he barked, the owners had to summon the thought, "thank you, but I've got this now", and correct him with a calm but firm 'shh'. I suggested they keep a bowl of dog treats by the front door and every time a visitor came to the house they were to drop a couple of the treats on the floor. The smell alone would be enough distraction to have Rivington sniffing them out, rather than barking at the guest. I wanted him to begin to associate visitors with positivity in place of nervousness.

Dogs change their behaviour as soon as their owners change theirs. With consistency, and by that I mean putting the changes into practice 100% of the time, Rivington will make a full recovery. He has already shown great progress.

You see the importance of being more dog?

But here's the thing. Being more dog does not solely mean thinking of things from your dog's point of view. It also means we should literally be more like our dogs (only once they are balanced).

It took me a while to learn and understand this and I hope you'll bear with me while I explain. In this book, I hope to pass on how we can live a happier life, not just by changing our dogs' behaviour into becoming that perfect companion, but by learning from our four legged friends – for they are experts in taking every hour as it comes, without fretting; they forgive in an instant; they love unconditionally.

There are many life lessons to be learnt from just being more like man's best friend, and once we can be more dog we can discover the secrets of what makes them (and ultimately us) so content.

"Expectation has brought me disappointment. Disappointment has brought me wisdom."

RASHEED OGUNLARU

❶
(NOT) MY STORY

I have not always been a dog behaviourist. For many years I had another job altogether and a different kind of life.

Let me take you back to the start of when it all changed.

A couple of years ago, I was woken by the doorbell and stumbled downstairs to answer it. It had been a late night the previous evening, at the launch party of a friend's new store, and the cocktails had run freely. It didn't help that they had been quite so delicious either, and my enthusiasm had run away with me. Thick headed, I opened the door. A man stood there in a blur. At first I attributed my inability to focus on the fact that I wasn't properly awake yet. We chatted briefly. He was a friend of my husband's, who had come to pick up a bag he had left behind the day before. He never did come into focus, and as we exchanged pleasantries, I started to panic inside. Why couldn't I see properly?

I don't wish to dwell on this scary chapter in my life, but I'll give a quick synopsis. I don't want to be bound by that story. I am not that story. I have moved on.

(As I write and dredge up these memories, my left eye is starting to twitch already. Our minds and bodies are linked as one, and mine seems super sensitive.)

The vision in my left eye was impaired. Everything I saw through it was a blur, a bit like trying on someone else's glasses who has a completely different prescription to yours. Although my right eye was fine, what I saw in general was discombobulating. My distance vision was particularly diminished. I sought immediate advice from an optometrist who prescribed glasses, which helped somewhat. They told me it was irreversible degeneration, to be expected in someone my age. The elasticity had gone, never to return. But what they could not explain was why my eyesight had changed so dramatically overnight.

Two days later the glasses no longer worked and I returned to have another prescription diagnosed. More panic. If things were to progress at this rate I would be blind within a week. A week later the prescription had indeed changed again – but this time it had improved. They double checked their readings. They had not come across this before. It should not technically be possible. The small glimmer of hope this gave me faded abruptly the next day when I was back to the previous week's readings. No-one could explain the yo-yoing. I was a mystery.

After several visits, and being told I would need glasses for life, I had acquired four different pairs of glasses, all with different prescriptions. This myopia was expensive business.

Every morning I would wake with my heart in my mouth. Was I going to be able to see better or worse? I became nervous about opening my eyes. I would immediately look out of the window at the same tree, and determine from its focus whether today was a good eye day or a bad eye day, and pick up the appropriate pair of glasses. I hated the varifocals. They made me feel dizzy and sick. I would quiz everyone I knew who wore glasses, how long it took to get used to them. Nobody else seemed to have a problem, which made me feel uneasy.

It wasn't simply the eyesight which had gone astray – the lack of vision led to a loss in confidence, and a general nervousness, and rabbit-in-the-headlights type behaviour. This constant anxiety caused a loss of appetite, and I became painfully thin. I'm a fairly slim build naturally, so losing weight was not a plus. Instead it was a further worry, to add to the spiral of other worries. I would force myself to eat, which is hard when you are not hungry, and I would manage only a few mouthfuls which would taste of cardboard, before I could eat no more.

My glasses became my crutch. Rather like a drug addict who finds he has lost his wrap and won't be able to get his next fix, I became panicky if I mislaid any pair, or didn't have all four pairs in my handbag at any one time.

Up until this point in my life, I had been a very independent and capable woman. My family would say I definitely wore the trousers! Now I was anxious, teary and clung to my husband like a pathetic child. I would ask him to take the driver's seat – metaphorically and physically. This is when he knew it must be serious for I *always* did the driving. I hated being left alone in the house and was relieved when he came home at the end of each day. I had no purpose to my days, and at weekends followed him on errands, and asked where he was going every time he left the house. On Saturdays we would go and watch our son play cricket. My son's shock of white blonde hair has always made him easy to pick out in a crowd, but now I couldn't decipher which boy he was on the pitch. All the boys were identical little blurs. So I just sat there looking into space.

I could not keep sitting around doing nothing, so I sought more advice. My husband had just left for a weekend away so I took myself in a cab to the eye hospital. I distinctly remember being blinded by the sunlight through my sobbing eyes, which sent the light off in shafts in all directions. I had become light sensitive too. (In the weeks that followed I became a bit like Dracula, only comfortable to come out at dusk.)

The eye doctors wanted to put drops into *both* eyes to dilate the pupils, which would blur my vision for a few hours. I panicked and refused. They finished their examination declaring that as far as they could see, without being able to make a comparison to the other eye, there was no physical damage, and all nerves were intact. So why couldn't I see properly? Still no answer.

I rang my husband from the waiting room. He was about to board his plane, but turned sharply around , abandoning his long awaited cycling trip, and came to sit beside me, wipe away the tears, and take me home. He was so amazing and kind and selfless, and I can't imagine having got through those months without him. His support has been invaluable ever since.

A Harley Street eye specialist was next on my list. The ophthalmologist assigned to my case tried to put me at ease, for I was a bag of nerves, but I found it rather unnerving being nose to nose with this stranger. As he peered deep into my eyes, I felt like he was boring into my very soul. He performed every test I had had before, and dozens more – hours of prodding and eyedrops and glaring lights, after which he announced, "You'll be pleased to hear there is no damage". Still no explanation.

It is here that I have to acknowledge my dear, wise mother. She is always on hand to lend a listening ear – it comes naturally to her, which is probably why she makes such a great psychotherapist. She has always been well ahead of her time in knowing that any ailment in our bodies is related to our thoughts. My siblings and I used to raise our eyebrows when she would 'prescribe' expressing yourself truly for tonsillitis, or being (mentally) more flexible, for joint pain. If you had a sore neck, it was more than likely that someone you knew was being a pain in the neck. Sort out your differences with them, and the pain would go away. With this ethos in mind she simply asked, "What is it you don't want to see?".

Answering this question would take several months, a colossal shift in attitude and habits, a change in career and some patient hounds.

*"To err is human
– to forgive is canine."*

ANON

2

BAGEL AND MELVIN: THE VALUE OF MISTAKES

The very first case I ever took on as a behaviourist was my cousin's dog. I wanted secure ground before I launched myself on the general public, so I asked her if I could use her as a case study. She had a 2 year old female beagle called Bagel, who was unpredictable with other dogs and had poor recall. It would chase and bark at larger dogs and not come back when called.

Beagles have a reputation for being fairly stubborn and hard to train, so my cousin had already employed a professional to guide her and improve Bagel's behaviour. She had put in six months dedicated work, and by the end of it had a pretty responsive dog on and off lead. However the setback came when Bagel was set upon in the park by a large dog. Not only this, but Bagel had also witnessed the dog she lived with get attacked by another large dog. No wonder she had become wary of large breeds and tried to see them off.

It is in a beagle's nature to bark and howl a lot. They are hunting dogs, and do this to alert the pack leader that prey has been sighted. Bagel was most likely using her natural instinct to alert her family that she had spotted something worth howling about. In this case, not so much prey, but threat.

My first mistake was taking Bagel out for a training walk without my cousin, so keen was I to get going. It is normal practice to do an assessment without the owner present, as dogs often act differently in the presence of their owners. However, I should have witnessed the way Bagel behaved with my cousin first: seen first hand the charging and barking, and watched how my cousin dealt with it. I would then have been in a better position to offer guidance.

Forgetting that essential bit of my training in my anxiety to impress, I went off to a quiet area of the park, and did some lead work to get Bagel to bond with me and get her responding to me, which she did nicely. We then sought out some other dogs. When several large dogs passed, I called her over to me and got her to look at me, not at the dogs. Problem diverted. Half an hour later and she still had not reacted to any other dog. I was stumped. Here was a perfect dog!

I returned to the house and reported back. But because my

cousin had not been present, she had not witnessed that her dog could be 'perfect' in the hands of another leader. I deduced that it was something about their relationship therefore that had to change, so I launched into spurting out all my knowledge: how I thought she could change how she was with the dog, how whatever energy you project determines how a dog behaves, how she must have been winding her up, how dogs don't display unwanted behaviours without reacting to our input in someway, and so on. She suddenly had a very important meeting to get to and I had to leave, tail between my legs.

(In retrospect I should have simply recommended some scent games for Bagel. Beagles love nothing more than to put their noses to the ground and follow a scent to a prize at the end. This may have been engagement enough to stop her scanning the horizon for 'prey'.)

I apologise to my cousin for my insensitivity, but thank her for being my first guinea pig, and for teaching me that knowing how to handle the humans is as important as how to handle the dogs.

Although I had learnt much from this first encounter, I had failed to give advice in such a way for it to be productive. I was going to have to change my approach.

Sometimes we can't learn unless we make a mistake first. As Maya Angelou (author and civil rights activist) said simply, "When you know better, you do better".

If I treat someone I love in a hostile manner, and they are more hurt than I expected them to be, I may regret my actions, but at least I have learnt to be softer next time. I learnt that I needed to be more diplomatic and less critical. Nobody welcomes criticism, and it only serves to shut down communication completely.

Just as I can't correct an aggressive dog unless he makes a mistake and shows his aggression, nor can I correct myself unless I mess up first. Learn, grow, and move on.

Whenever crisis rears its head these days, I am now able to think, "What are you here to teach me, crisis?", instead of automatically switching to my old default position of falling apart.

I have lost count of the times that an owner has apologised for their dog barking at me or for lunging at another dog when under my control. I have to explain that I need the mistakes to happen so I can take the appropriate action to curb that behaviour.

One such time was with Melvin, a wirey old terrier. He was extremely protective of his female owner. He wouldn't even let her husband come near her, let alone visitors to the house. When I arrived, Melvin barked at me, but I didn't let him gather too much pace, and went directly to go and sit next to his female owner on the sofa, whilst giving him the 'you're not going to mess with me' eye. I think he was so shocked by my purposeful move, that he just curled up quietly at her feet. They were quite in awe. As was I to be honest! Some way into my chat about calm assertive energy, Melvin jumped onto the sofa beside her uninvited. I gently pushed his rear and told him 'off'. He got down, but then unused to being challenged, took a full lunge at my leg.

They say you haven't really 'arrived' as a behaviourist, until you've joined the bite club, so secretly I was kind of pleased. He was my 47th case, so long time coming. I immediately stood and took a pace towards him to show him that his aggressive behaviour was not going to have the desired effect he wanted of making the threat go away. Barking and biting was not going to work any more. He had to choose a different option – surrender to the moment.

After that he was putty in my hands, but the challenge was going to be enabling the husband to do the same. Husband and wife had to show a united front and assert the same rules. I left them with some exercises to practise. They were embarrassed and apologetic about the bite but I was very proud of my purple bruise, which lingered for a week or so to remind me to be thankful to the dog that misbehaved in my presence, and not to view it as a negative.

Mistakes whether made by dogs or humans, are invaluable. Without misbehaviour there would be no redemption.

With continual corrections of ourselves (and our dogs), the mistakes gradually happen less and less as we grow and learn. Just recognising we have made a mistake is progress, so we don't have to be too hard on ourselves when we mess up. Thank the mistake, and move on. This is easy to say, but harder to do.

I went through a fair bit of angst after the case involving my cousin, before my mind was at rest. I hadn't yet learnt a dog's great skill of leaving the past behind me.

Recognising when your Dog is not Balanced

A balanced dog is a happy dog.

If he is displaying any of the symptoms listed below, you might want to enlist a behaviourist who can help in his rehabilitation:

- Excessive barking
- Separation anxiety – can't leave your side without protesting
- Aggression to other dogs or humans
- Toileting in the house (adult dogs)
- Destructiveness – chewing up your house
- Fearful or anxious. Phobias – this could be fear of going outside, loud noises, men etc.
- Obsessions – self chewing, tail chasing, toy fixation, pacing, carpet licking
- Hyper activity

My biggest mistake, before I learnt to be more dog, was somewhat a contributor to getting me into the situation I was in with my eye.

One of my larger projects in my previous career (as an interior designer) involved a particularly demanding client. He had asked for my help to redesign a house he was renting. He wanted to completely redecorate the east wing from scratch and build a kitchen extension and a barn in the garden. (Yes I did say *renting.*) This slowly stretched to making changes to every room in the house. Normally this would be absolutely fine – it's what I did for a living. But there was something about this man that did not sit well with me. He had too much money and too little respect for his staff. I soon learnt that his nanny and previous interior designer had both recently resigned, and his PA handed in her notice a few weeks after I had been working with him. This should, of course, have set alarm bells ringing. But instead, every time he asked me to change something I had already done, I replied, "Yes, no problem", wanting to be totally professional, wanting to be the one that delivered, while inside I was screaming "No! Enough!" I don't mean he was changing his mind about a triviality like paint colour: I would furnish an entire wing, have tiles laid, wallpaper up, cabinetry designed etc and he would have me return furniture, pull up the newly laid tiles, strip the wallpaper and redesign the joinery, on a whim.

He rang me once on a Sunday and demanded an immediate meeting. I said I was busy but could do first thing Monday morning.

"It's *you* who has to fit in with *me*", he replied, "Not the other way round".

You'll be pleased to hear I did not cave. The urgent Monday morning meeting came, and he was out. He arrived 45 minutes late with no apology. Was this his way of getting his own back?

Yes I was billing him by the hour, but the process of being disrespected and doing everything twice or sometimes 3 times over, was totally soul destroying and sapped me of energy. I sacrificed my physical health to be known as a highly competent individual. I did not lay down any boundaries, which was my mistake, and he took advantage of that. I would have had so much more respect from him if I had simply said no.

My eye went weird the following week. Was it him I did not want to see? I certainly thought so at the time.

"It becomes very obvious, by reading a dog, how stable or unstable his human companion is. Our dogs are our mirrors."

CESAR MILLAN

3

NINJA: HOW TO GAIN RESPECT AND LEAD FROM THE FRONT

I needed to change my ways if I was not going to be walked all over. If I didn't respect myself, how could I expect anyone else to respect me? I didn't know how to at the time, and I fell a fair way before I could get out of the hole I was in, but I would learn a valuable lesson from my second ever case study, almost a year after I had ditched that demanding client.

Ninja was my brother's dog. I was keeping it in the family for now as I was still not ready for the masses. She is an unusual breed, a Portuguese water dog, often mistaken for a poodle mix. She was only six months old but already up to my knees. 'Ninja' brings to mind a highly trained, composed and skilful warrior; obedient and calm yet always ready for some rough and tumble. Never has there been a greater juxtaposition. Ninja was a big floppy softy, with no regard for rules. But she was still learning what was expected of her. Her main trait was pulling whoever was the other end of the lead down the street.

My brother and his family and I arrived in the park. (I asked him to be a case study incidentally, not the other way round. He went along with it for my sake, but didn't expect any miracles.) I distinctly remember the sound of laughter as I took a lead-chewing and jumping Ninja on a training walk. I knew from my experience with my cousin that my brother had to witness a result in order to change his opinion, so I soldiered on. I changed direction often so as to keep Ninja on her toes, and responding to me. I stopped to get eye contact every now and again, without using my voice. The less said the better the response. **If any dog is to follow you, you must gain its trust and respect first.**

Once I had Ninja under control, I handed the lead to my ten year old nephew . He is kind and soft hearted and not as physical as his younger brothers and struggled to keep Ninja in check. I had to change him into a leader. I asked him who the most annoying boy in school was, and told him to imagine what he would tell the boy if he were headmaster. He had to be firm but fair. All he needed to do was assume this role in his head. He also had to assume the posture of a leader, as dogs are constantly watching our body language (and that of other dogs). How would his headmaster stride across the playground? So it was shoulders back, chin up, and look forward, not down at the dog. He took on the role brilliantly and his dog responded to the new energy she felt on the other end of the lead. She stopped mucking around and started following his directions.

It took just 10 minutes to have boy and dog walking politely side by side. My brother by now had changed his quizzical look into a slow nod.

Energy is the single most important thing in the dog world, and we can mirror this energy in our own lives to bring about respect. I don't mean energy in the sense of how much stamina you have, but energy as in what kind of aura you are projecting.

Dogs do not follow bossy or weak energy, or a loveable leader. This means that no amount of soft persuasion or yelling will get them to do what you ask. This may work in the human world – you may force an employee to obey, but it will not gain you any respect. Dogs need a calm assertive leader, and this is the leader we should all aspire to be, with our dogs, and with each other. It's the sort of leadership that gets results. In the wild, dogs will naturally follow the strongest, calmest pack member. Their survival depends upon that leader making the right decisions. They will chase away any weak members of the pack, for those weaklings will jeopardise the pack's safety. So it's no surprise then that owners who shout at and punish their dogs or, at the other end of the scale, who exercise no rules and discipline, have the most problematic dogs. If we take dogs out of their natural wild habitat and into our homes, we must be for them what they naturally need – a pack leader – in order for them to live balanced lives.

If a dog goes through the door in front of you, and walks down the street ahead of you, he is leading the walk. He is making all the decisions: "I'll stop to sniff here", "I'll pick up the pace because I see something appealing over there". This is a clue that he does not view you as his leader, and subsequently most likely he will not always do as you tell him. Making decisions can be stressful for a dog. They need to be able to relax in the knowledge that all decisions will be made for them.

Dogs read energy. They are not concerned about how cool you are or how powerful you are. They will still pee on your carpet if they do not respect you. Energy is felt more by animals and children than by adults. They are not fooled by our acting, not influenced by our status, job or appearance. They see through all of that to the true you.

It's important to know what *level* of energy you are too. High, medium, low? When choosing a dog instead of asking 'what breed of dog' we want, you would do well to ask 'what level of energy' dog do we want? Get a dog to match your energy. The dog will suss out your energy level in minutes, and if you are not compatible, there may be trouble ahead.

Ninja was a high energy dog, so she needed a high energy owner to help her drain some of her excitability and exuberance on a daily basis. Without an outlet for her energy, Ninja may have turned to destructiveness or obsessive behaviour.

She had a habit of jumping up on people, which was part of her venting some of her energy, but in the wrong way. In the wild, a dog would never jump up on another dog at a first meeting. It is a huge mark of disrespect, and would probably be met with a growl. But we encourage it, by petting them while they have their paws on us, so they believe this is desired behaviour as they are being rewarded for it. (Then we shout at them when we are wearing white trousers and they have muddy feet and do the same. How confused they must be.) Getting your dog to respect you means setting some boundaries, and the first boundary you should address is your personal space.

This is a lesson I have taken into my life with humans too. I have learnt to set up soft boundaries towards people who I feel may be taking advantage of me. In fact, I made it my new year's resolution to be able to say 'no' more often. The results are quite remarkable.

How to be your Dog's Pack Leader

Ultimately, a dog should be able to be relaxed, knowing he has no decisions to make. Leaving your dog to make decisions, often the wrong ones, can lead to him becoming stressed or unbalanced. Dogs love rules!

1. Always be calm and assertive. Dogs do not follow weak energy or shouting.
2. Set some rules and stick to them 100% of the time, otherwise the one time you lapse, your dog will no longer take you seriously, and you will be back to square one.
3. Use positive reinforcement. Do not punish.
4. Leave the house, ie walk out the door, in front of your dog. If he goes out first, he is already leading the walk. You are the leader, he is the follower. Have him walk beside you, not in front of you, on the lead.
5. Do not allow jumping up on you . This would never happen in the wild and is a huge mark of disrespect. He can only come up when you invite him to.

6. I discourage owners from allowing dogs to sleep in their beds. In the wild, the pack leader would have the best sleeping position, and would not share it with any of his pack. If you cannot bear to be parted from your pooch (and this will be your need, not his), then make sure he leaves his spot when you roll over, and jumps off the bed when you tell him to.

7. Do not feed your dog from the table. Food is the greatest commodity in the wild, and the pack leader would never share any of his food with the pack. Your dog will be less likely to follow your commands if he does not view you as the leader.

8. Make your dog work for his food. He may not have to hunt for his food, but he should have to work for it. Take him for a walk first. Ask him to sit and stay as you put the bowl down. Waiting (psychological work) is key. Do not give food to your dog unless he is in a calm submissive state. If you have multiple dogs, feed the calmest first.

9. Set boundaries. Ownership of territory is primal for a pack leader in the wild, and they will mark out their space. Your dog should not be allowed everywhere in your house – upstairs, on the sofa, on or in your bed, in the baby's room. At least not without an invitation.

10. Protect your dog. Step in if another dog is harassing yours. He has to know you are in control of the situation if he is going to trust you and follow your leadership.

11. And incidentally, all the humans in the house should be the pack leader. There is no pecking order.

"If we learn to Control our Mind and Listen to our Souls we can consciously choose to be Joyful instead of sad."

NATASA PANTOVIC NUIT

4

ODIN: FOCUS AND PATIENCE

The experience of redesigning my wealthy client's house over and over had left me in a weakened state, mentally and physically. I was drained. At first I blamed him and the stress he had caused me for my lack of vision. But this proved too simplistic. I was forced to give up my work as an interior designer. I couldn't look at a computer without getting a headache and eye strain. I couldn't look at my phone. I couldn't watch TV or read a book. I got sensory overload when looking at supermarket shelves – too many products, too many labels. The same happened during a trip to an art fair. All those bright lights and patterns and colours made me dizzy, and had me diverting my gaze to the floor for visual relief. I spent the rest of the exhibition in the café staring melancholically into my cup of coffee.

I was having regular attacks of anxiety, and still clung to

my husband for support. I couldn't do anything physical, as I felt so exhausted all the time. My weekly game of tennis, which I had loved, was definitely off the cards, as was yoga, which would have been beneficial for calming my nerves. I couldn't even muster up the energy to garden. I walked around in a kind of daze. My body was trying to send me a message: stop everything! It forced me into it, as I wasn't listening. I was completely worn out.

One night I went round to a girlfriend's house for a change of scenery. Doing nothing and seeing no one was very dull. She started to prepare supper, and thoughtfully put on a humorous show on tv to cheer me up. It was one that I could understand without having to look at the screen. She served up a steaming plate of pasta just 10 minutes later to find me fast asleep on her sofa.

Something had to change. I couldn't go on like this.

On the advice of my mother, I went to see a psychotherapist. If my vision was linked to something going on in my head, it was worth a try. So far I had been trying to treat the symptom, not the cause of my poor vision. Wearing glasses may have helped somewhat, but without getting to the 'why' the vision went, there would be no improvement.

The therapist asked me what I wanted to achieve with the sessions, and I replied, "To be able to sit in this chair and look at you without my glasses." I couldn't understand why she wouldn't let me come every day. Surely then my vision would come back quicker? Patience has never been one of my attributes.

She spent the first session asking about my parents and my childhood. Before we had even touched upon the present day, the hour was up and it would be a week until I could even talk about how I was feeling *right now,* because that was the problem, surely?

She was actually better than I wanted to give her credit for. During one of our weekly sessions she hit the jackpot. I burst into tears when I mentioned my daughter was going to start boarding for 6th form. Where did that come from? My son was already boarding, so up until now we had enjoyed just my daughter's chirpy company every evening after school. Was it that I was so upset by her going away? After all I would still see her every weekend. Or was it that I was terrified at the prospect of recalibrating the relationship with my husband? She had me thinking. (Little did I know at this stage that it was the thinking that would inhibit my healing process.) Damn! I so thought I had addressed and dealt with this empty nest thing. Apparently not. So was this the future I literally did not want to see?

My route to therapy took me on the Westway going in to central London. One morning the road was blocked. Police were in abundance and there was thick black smoke in the air. I stared in horror at the smouldering tower block. I never made it to therapy, but probably had one of the most thought provoking afternoons in spite of this.

Those helpless victims of Grenfell had no more future, and their families would forever be emotionally scarred. My problems were put horribly into perspective.

Instead of focusing on what was wrong with me, I started to focus on what would bring me joy (which obviously didn't involve computers, phones or tvs). Unwittingly, I was following the spiritual teacher Eckhart Tolle's doctrine all by myself – taking my attention to well being, not illness, for **what we focus on grows**.

I still had low energy, but I could use my ears and mouth no problem. My friends downloaded audio books and podcasts for me on to my phone, (I still couldn't look at it without getting a headache), and I became a fan of Desert Island Discs, which I had originally assumed was just for old people. They changed the font size on my phone to 'ridiculously large', and the clever ones texted me with caps lock on, or not at all.

I sought out a choir. I've always enjoyed singing, even though not particularly good at it, so when one advertised 'no auditions required', I was in. But as lovely as the people were, the music was a bit dour and I had to sight read the pages and pages of scores, with great strain on my eyes. Then without looking any further, the answer came to me. A musical friend of mine, or rather I should say, a friend of mine who likes musicals, had always wanted to try out gospel singing. She researched a local group and asked me to go along for moral support. I went for her sake but had no intention of attending more than the one session. I ended up going every week and to date I have performed in several of their concerts. All songs were taught by ear and repetition. No written music sheets required. It was perfect for me, and so uplifting. This was powerful, high energy stuff, and a smile would often creep over my face, as we swayed in unison, clapping from side to side. I didn't need to believe in God, I just needed to believe that singing my heart out, was good for the soul. The shoe seemed to fit.

With no job (I was not well enough to return to work), I had to fill my days with something other than obsessing about me. I enrolled in a sculpture course at a local art school. It was just one day a week, but gave me something to focus on.

We were sculpting live nudes out of clay. Our first model was a lanky black male dancer. He unrobed in front of us and took up his pose confidently on the couch. He had delicious shiny skin and undulating muscles that belonged in the pages of a glossy magazine. His appendage was predictable!

Acting as if we saw this kind of vision every day of our lives, we very nonchalantly busied ourselves slapping clay onto clay and measuring up. After around 20 minutes of remaining statuesque, the model took his first break and left the room to stretch his legs. We girls in the room looked up and eyed one another sheepishly (for we hadn't yet spoken to one another) before almost simultaneously letting out a breathy "Phwooooar!" The room erupted into hysterics. It was a wonderfully childish moment and, I realised, the first time I had laughed in months. This was the medicine I needed.

At the end of day one, I was pleased with my finished piece. It bore some resemblance and had held my attention utterly focused for 7 hours. It had been a kind of meditation. I had not once thought about my eyes, or the past or the future. **I was totally living in the moment, and it was intoxicating.** I would later be able to draw parallels from this, with dogs, who without exception live only in the present, and are therefore more able than most humans to stay content with what is. A skill I was yet to fully learn.

Having declared my piece finished, I was told that we were working with the same model in the same pose until half term – for a further 5 full days. My heart sank slightly, for as gorgeous as he was, I wanted to move on. Achieve more. Patience was again being flagged as my weak point. But our tutor showed me how I could improve my sculpture, how my proportions were slightly out, how I could show the muscle structure under the flesh. I'm grateful to him, as I did rework my piece and it did transform rather remarkably. I actually only lasted on this piece for another 3 sessions out of the 5 before I knocked up another one. This focus and patience thing was a slow learning curve for me.

The things we are worst at (patience in my case) tend to get thrown at us again and again until we learn from them. This was my first glimpse that slowing down could have positive effects; a trait that I have dragged kicking and screaming into my current life. **I could not train a dog (or its owners), without the utmost patience**.

Results cannot always be expected after a single session. Some behaviours are so ingrained that it takes a lot of repetition to correct the old habits and instil the new.

Odin was a young male staffie, and typical to type, he was aggressive with other dogs. The Staffordshire bull terrier was originally bred for bull baiting and dog fighting, so it's no surprise that some of these tendencies still show themselves today. In Germanic mythology, Odin was a revered God of battle, victory and death. This wasn't helping poor Odin the dog. Anyone with any knowledge of his name would immediately associate him with destruction and negativity, and coupled with the muzzle he wore , would back away before getting to know him. This only serves to make the dog feel powerful, and breeds more negative behaviour. When I first met Odin's owner, I was a little wary. Weathered and unshaven, he wore army style trousers and a reflective jacket, and was restraining his dog on a thick metal chain lead, wrapped twice round his hand. All the dog needed was a studded collar to complete the stereotype. (It was wrong of me to prejudge him – a habit that I am trying to kick.)

I started by switching the lead to a piece of rope loosely looped around the dog's neck. I instructed the owner to hold it between 2 fingers only. It only took a couple of corrections (short sharp tug) to get Odin to understand what we wanted from him. Without the tension on the lead, he no longer felt the need to pull. I noticed that the dog never looked at his owner. Never glanced up at him for direction or approval. There was no connection here. His focus was continually scanning the horizon for prey. **Eye contact is key to getting your dog to respect you.** If he avoids looking at you then that is a clue he is not paying attention to you and does not perceive you as the leader.

I advised the owner to start feeding Odin by hand, little by little, and to wait until his dog looked him in the eye before he gave the next mouthful. On walks also he was to stop regularly and get eye contact before continuing.

Odin had a muzzle order against him. He had attacked a couple of dogs, and the police had got involved. One more strike and he was out. His life was in my hands. I believed it was possible to get the order revoked, but it would take time, patience and consistency. People took one look at the muzzle and the breed, and moved aside like the parting of the Red Sea. This made my task harder, as I needed contact with other dogs for his rehabilitation.

Just as there is no source of darkness, only a source of light, I knew that dogs (and people), are not born bad. The good is always there, it just needed bringing to the fore.

The 'light' had just been obscured, a bit like the sun above a stormy sky. Odin was a good dog underneath it all, he just needed guidance.

We used clicker training to mark the *good* behaviour, ie walking past a dog without reacting, and he responded well to it. (A clicker is a little hand held gizmo which you press to make a click sound every time the dog does something you approve of. After each click you then give a little food reward. It's a highly effective way of asserting positive behaviour). If what we focus on grows, then we had to focus on the good behaviour, not the bad. Odin soon learnt that listening for the clicker and getting snacks was far more rewarding than the 'high' he might have been getting from attacking other dogs. We taught him some agility, and some new tricks, which all helped to have him paying attention to his owner, and not the rest of the park. My first impressions of Odin's owner could not have been more wrong. He saw me on a weekly basis and worked daily on improving his dog's behaviour. He listened to my advice, took it on board, and followed through. He was courteous and steadfast, and willing to do whatever it took to make his dog happy and balanced.

He did not expect overnight success. Every time there was an incident and Odin lunged at another dog, we took a step back and started over. His patience pulled through and Odin's aggression became less and less, and it was a joy to watch the bond between the two of them get stronger and stronger. Yes there have been setbacks, but Odin's owner is a master of patience and positive thinking and this will have a direct effect on his dog.

Better results are achieved when you focus on the good, slow down and get a firm foundation. Don't rush to find a cure. This was a lesson it took me a long time to figure out in relation to my own life.

Dog Breed Tendencies

Understand that your dog may be performing the way its instinct is telling it to. Do not be surprised or angry when your dog exhibits behaviour it was bred for.

You may have to create activities to channel these natural impulses, otherwise their pent up frustration will lead to behavioural problems. In short, dogs need jobs.

- Terriers like to dig. Do not be surprised if your garden is full of holes if they have no other outlet for their behaviour. They have acute hearing, highly tuned for listening to the slightest noise or movement underground. Bury their favourite toy or a bone in the bottom of your garden, or a park, and have them dig it out.
- Retrievers like to fetch. Do not be annoyed if your dog goes after every other dog's ball in the park. Play any number of throwing games with them. But don't make it too easy – throw into water, into bushes, and have them sniff it out. Play games in the home which have them picking up and clearing away their toys.

- Sight hounds such as lurchers, greyhounds and afghans, like to chase. They have been bred to hunt by sight, rather than scent. They need to run flat out for short bursts at top speed. They will have strong prey drive and want to chase every squirrel and cat on the block, unless you channel this natural energy. Throwing a ball for them, or better still, google "lure coursing" and find a local club, where they can chase an artificial hare (the lure).
- Herders like collies and heelers like to herd. It would be natural for them to bark at and run round bikes and joggers or small children playing. Give them an outlet for this by playing frisbee or football, and get them jumping and doing agility, or enroll in a flyball club.
- Scenthounds like beagles, dachshunds and bloodhounds love to track. They often have their noses permanently to the ground and have bags of stamina. Drain their energy by playing hide and seek, getting them to sniff you out, or hiding their toys around the house, or learn how to play drag hunting games.
- Scent hounds are often very vocal – alerting the pack to a scent they have picked up, so it's important you curb this urge early on with a firm "shh".

- Fighting breeds like bulldogs, pitbulls, Staffordshire bull terriers were bred to guard livestock and people and to fight for sport. They are naturally stubborn and don't react to pain the way other breeds do. They need an assertive owner.
- Protection dogs like German shepherds and dobermans were bred to guard, and challenge humans. It's really important for them to have a firm handler. They enjoy tug of war games, but teach them to release on command, or you will find them feeling they can dominate you.
- Huskies and mountain dogs (St Bernard, Bernese mountain dog) have a tendency to pull on the lead. They were bred to pull sleighs and carts. With the correct harness, have them pull you on rollerblades or a scooter.
- Lap dogs such as the bichon frise, pug and chihuahua were bred as human companions, so they are more susceptible to separation anxiety and possessiveness over their owner than other breeds. It's important they are exposed to 'happy' periods of time on their own if they are to remain balanced.

"I have never met a dog I couldn't help; however I have met humans who were unwilling to change"

CESAR MILLAN

5

PURDEY: NOTHING CHANGES WITHOUT MAKING A CHANGE

I was still searching for answers about my health. Armed with the probability that my lack of vision and overall weariness was down to my fear of the future, I threw myself into finding alternative healthcare that might help. I notched up a good many 'ists': psychologist, acupuncturist, reflexologist, intuitive therapist, spiritual response therapist, kinesiologist, and a homeopath for good measure.

Once again, patience not being my strong point, and with such a drive to be 'fixed', I chucked everything at the problem. Little did I know at this point that the only way to move forward, was by being just where I was! It was only when I surrendered to my situation that I would start to see any changes.

A friend of mine had been to see a spiritual healer and psychic who had worked wonders for her, so I booked an appointment. Florina was a petite, softly spoken lady in whose presence I felt immediate warmth and security. She did all the talking – such a relief after all those hours spilling my guts in the psychologist's chair – and I melted into her words. She intuitively knew much about me. Not so much hard facts, but feelings. She had a picture in her head of dancing and music in the family. There is never a Saturday night in our house without my daughter or husband cranking up the tunes and dancing round the kitchen. She could sense that I was creative, and had a love of animals. I told her I had a dog who I loved very much. "But your dog has something wrong with its eye too", she replied. And she was quite right. My dog had developed an eye infection in her left eye which was lingering more than it should. Florina suggested that my dog was trying to 'take on' my illness, and hence take it away from me. (It's actually widely known that dogs whose owners have cancer, often develop cancer themselves, in a bid to rid their owners of the disease. They also have the ability to sniff out cancers even before some of the most sophisticated equipment is able to do so.) I had never thought to link my eye with my dog's eye, but maybe it was no coincidence that both our left eyes were affected.

Almost immediately Florina reassured me that my vision would come back. How long it took would be up to me. At last, something I wanted to hear. She put her hands over my eyes and I felt the most incredible heat, and saw dancing purple lights in front of my closed eyes. It was not the miracle I had hoped for, but healing had begun. First I had to change myself. She told me that I should stop searching for answers, stop seeing all the 'ists', and be thankful every day for my perfect life and my perfect eyes. I told her I did not like my eyes. They are small and piggy, and no amount of eye makeup makes me feel any more in love with them. She was shocked. "But Fenella, just think what they do for you!"

And she was right. How shallow of me to have been berating their physical appearance while they worked so hard to bring me happiness, which I had not even attributed to them. I had only just been telling Florina about the incredible beauty of the Alps in springtime. She had told me to mentally go there as my 'happy place' when I felt panic rising. My eyes were helping me in ways I didn't understand, until now. I began to totally reassess my relationship with my eyes.

Florina gave me the courage to go out and face the world. She made me feel safe and a little braver each time I saw her. I had several sessions with her over the following months, and the one thing that sticks in my mind is her saying, "They are telling me to tell you not to go back to your old ways". And so far I haven't.

In fact, to remind myself to stay on the right path, without having to use endless post-it notes round the house, I went for the more indelible solution of getting a tattoo: a Sanskrit symbol representing a mantra which reminds us that all living things are connected, and no one thing is more important than the next. It keeps me grounded and humble and thankful, and I see it every day. (Tattoo age 49 – talk about a mid life crisis!)

My psychotherapist recommended a couple of books to me, which have become my bibles. The first is Eckhart Tolle's 'The Power of Now', which can be summed up fairly well in one sentence: 'All we have is the now, so why not enjoy it?'. The past is gone, the future never arrives; we only have the present. Worrying about the past (often a habit of people who suffer from depression), or the future (often a habit of people who suffer from anxiety), is wasted thoughts and wasted energy. Tolle speaks at length about the ego, which he defines as the image we have of ourselves as attached to status, possessions, race, religion, ability, physical appearance, job etc. But this is not our true self. Our true self is that which lives in the present moment and is not influenced by these things, and does not judge.

So if I could enjoy the now, and stop fretting about the future (like dogs incidentally), then I could summon up some peace from within.

Tolle spent 2 years sitting on park benches "in a state of deep bliss", just watching the world go by. This was after he almost committed suicide whilst studying for his doctorate. So often one achieves the best satisfaction after a period of great dissatisfaction and distress. I didn't know it yet, but this is what I was to experience.

The second book I rely on these days is 'A Woman's Best Medicine', which extolls the virtues of ayurvedic medicine. I was a little hung up about my health to say the least, so this recommendation was intended to show me how easy it was to maintain health mentally, physically and spiritually. The thought behind treating someone ayurvedically is that you are treating the whole person (mind, body and spirit) and not just the symptom. It is an ancient Hindu holistic (meaning whole body) system of healing. If the bodymind (talked of as one entity) is in harmony with the universe, you are likely to have good health. If something disrupts this balance, you might well get sick. Things which can disrupt this balance are genetic defects, seasonal changes, diet, age and emotions. My balance was clearly out of kilter (interestingly, a word derived from English dialect 'kelter', literally meaning 'good health'). I was ever so slowly learning how to put it back into kilter.

Modern medicine is geared towards treating the symptom, rather than getting rid of the root cause. The medicine may mask the symptoms for a while, but they will most likely re-occur, and you might even get some nasty side effects to boot. While modern medicine gives everyone who suffers from, say heartburn, the same synthetic medicine, Ayurveda will give each person a different remedy based on their personal make-up, and it is all natural, with no side effects, and long lasting results. (A bit like homeopathy.) It also treats the mind, which in turn helps physical symptoms clear up on their own.

Some years ago, my daughter was concerned about some spots she was getting and asked me to take her to the doctor. I knew this was probably just hormones and it would pass of its own accord, but to put her mind at rest I took her along. I wanted her to hear it from a professional. The GP prescribed a very strong cream. I noticed the side effects were burning, itching and possible worsening of the condition. She said if the cream didn't work, she could prescribe a long course of antibiotics (which would effect her body's toxicity, and bacterial resistance to the drug in future), or put her on the contraceptive pill. She was 14 years old. She didn't mention – perhaps there was no time – the importance of a healthy diet, drinking water regularly, exercising or finding a way to manage stress. I marched my daughter out of there, unhappy at what I had heard, or rather not heard. I treated her ayurvedically with turmeric which is a powerful anti inflammatory and some other herbal cures, and we talked about diet and the importance of destressing. The outbreaks cleared up within a couple of weeks, never to return.

In my experience, effective medicine comes in many forms: music, nature, diet, exercise, positive thinking, a loving family, laughter, fresh air, friends, massage, breathing, relaxation.

It is such a shame that western medicine has not caught on. It would save the NHS a lot of money.

It was whilst reading 'A Woman's Best Medicine' that I knew I should recommend it to a great friend of mine who was recovering from chemotherapy. By nature a very grounded and intelligent individual, I wasn't convinced what Sarah's reaction would be, especially since she had been pumped full of chemical medicines, and they seemed to be doing the job. But she totally got it, and this was to be the start of many collaborations during our joint healing process.

We used to meet regularly just to chat really as we couldn't do much else. It felt ok to be doing nothing as long as someone else was doing nothing with me. She was full of positivity about her recuperation, and taught me a valuable tool to help me do the same. She told me to ignore any pain or anxiety, and to write down just one thing every day that brought me pleasure. It could be as simple as seeing a beautiful butterfly, or enjoying a hot bath. This was my very first experience of the beneficial effects of positive thinking. Little did I know then that it would become a way of life for me.

I recall one morning a get-together at her house for a coffee. She was wearing a stripey jumper and it was making my eyes go funny to the point that I couldn't look at her. She shuffled upstairs to change and in a dramatic Captain Oates fashion, and said with a flourish, 'I may be some time', as she had even less energy than me. What a pair we were! But at least we could laugh about it.

Laughter, I later learnt, is the best prescription for good health. Here's the science bit – it triggers the release of endorphins, which help your mind and body feel more relaxed. Hormones such as dopamine and neuropeptides are released, improving your mood and your response to stress and disease. One of the keys to my recovery was to find joy, not only in day to day things, but in my work and hobbies as well.

On my quest for alternative healthcare practitioners, my sister-in-law put me in touch with a man who seemed to have worked miracles on her and her friends, so much so that she called him 'Magic' Martin. She couldn't explain exactly what he did, save that he released blocked energy, and it worked. I was still willing to try anything.

It turned out that Martin was a kinesiologist working in a windowless back room of a health food store in Newbury. Not the setting I imagined for someone who purportedly should be healing the Hollywood stars of LA. He resembled my idea of a nutty professor, with his long grey hair and glasses, but far more measured and calm. He had a wonderful matter of fact way about him, and didn't care what anyone thought of him. In this sense, he was free. He told me he couldn't remember the last time he'd been ill, and it was largely this attitude that helped him achieve this. He didn't adhere to the rules society put on us, or bend to public opinion. How liberating. If only I too could just let go.

I was in there for 90 minutes, lying on a couch with my arms in the air, like a supine zombie sleepwalker, as he asked my subconscious a series of questions, and my body replied. ('Yes' for a strong arm and 'no' for a weak arm.) Sounds nuts. To redirect the flow of energy, and hence allow my body to heal itself, he had me performing a range of extraordinary tasks: making V signs to ward off my 'enemies', drawing symbols in the air with my finger, looking through red tinted glasses and rubbing lapis lazuli oil onto my nipples! (These were not all undertaken in the same session.) I think if he'd asked me to dance down the street naked singing the national anthem in Russian, I would have given it a shot.

It was totally bonkers, and I kept imagining there must be hidden cameras in the room and that I would shortly be seen to appear on an episode of 'Impractical Jokers'.

But joking aside, and without going into too much personal detail, it was pretty emotional in there. I had several fits of sobbing, and one of laughter.

He instantly knew which part of my eye wasn't functioning properly, by putting his hand over it and feeling the energy. He inferred that I should do less. "We are human BEings, not human DOings". Doing nothing and just being was ok. It was what I needed to heal. It echoed Florina and

Tolle's words. (My mum told me once that if you hear the same advice from two or more different sources, then it's probably true). So I finally started to listen. Although every bone in my body was screaming at me to do as much as I could to get better, not to do nothing. I had always been an achiever, and ironically this wanting to always achieve had led to my demise, so the change I needed was to stop striving. Martin unblocked some stagnant energy and rebooted my chakras. (I'm still learning what those are.) He sent me off with a much greater understanding of myself and the world around me. I learnt that the left side of our bodies is the feminine side, and the right is masculine, so any ailment on the left, in this case my left eye, would be associated with a female, in this case, my daughter. With relief I heard for the second time that my sight would recover.

But if I wanted change to come about, I had to make a change. That meant stop looking for answers, and do nothing. **Accept my situation for what it was.**

I didn't have to enjoy it, just accept it. If we do not make changes, we get stuck in the same old cyclical patterns.

Let me use a dog case to demonstrate this.

With a little bit of confidence under my belt, I decided to ask a dear old friend of mine if I could use her dog as a case study. We had been at school together, and had kept in touch ever since. She had had a hard time of it in the last few years, and had experienced multiple bereavements, poor health, and was struggling to keep her business afloat. She was headmistress of her own school, which both my children had attended. She has a way of engaging children like no other, in and out of the classroom. She has a modern day Mary Poppins air about her, and I would never dream of misbehaving in one of her classes. She can command a roomful of three year olds with wit, calm confidence, understanding yet firmness, and diversion if necessary, but she was unable to use the same skills on her dog.

Purdey is a feisty 2 year old jack russell with a host of classic symptoms: very poor recall (not coming back when called), pulling on the lead, aggression towards other dogs, obsessiveness over toys, chewing up the furniture, prey drive (chasing anything that moved), toileting in other people's houses etc, etc.

I asked my friend to summon up her inner teacher whilst on training sessions. This way she would be giving off the same confident 'no nonsense' energy she used in the classroom, which I was hoping Purdey would respond to, just like her school children did. Understandably, at the end of a long working day, my friend wanted to come home and switch off the leadership role, and relax in the company of her dog, and unwind, forgoing any rules. Purdey was not just a dog to her, but had to fill the role of partner, child and friend. She needed to be able to not only muck around and play with her, but also to pour her heart out to her. However, relying on the dog to fulfill her emotional needs, rather than the other way round, was counterproductive.

Just like children, dogs need instruction, rules, boundaries, limitations and consistency in order to feel safe and balanced. This is what Purdey was missing.

My friend and I met in the park for a couple of informal training sessions, and Purdey showed great promise. She is a bright dog, and keen to learn. I also had Purdey to stay for a week whilst my friend was on holiday, and this was a wonderful opportunity for me to give the dog some consistent leadership. By the end of her stay she was not chasing birds, not barging through the door before me, not jumping on my furniture, dropping the ball on command, giving me her paw on command, walking beautifully on the lead and coming back when I called. Result. I don't mean to blow my own trumpet, but just to demonstrate what can be achieved in a short space of time, with some dedication. But man did I put in the hours. I have never met a dog with such high energy. After a forty five minute run beside the bike (this being the third walk of the day), she would barely be panting, while I was exhausted. I expected her to get home and curl up and sleep after being fed, but instead she ran round the garden in circles and entertained herself with her ball, for some time afterwards. She never did chew any of my belongings, which was something, but I think that's because I challenged her enough mentally between walks (playing brain games) for her not to have much steam left to be bothered. This was a super high energy dog, and she needed an owner to match. She drained me after only a few days, so new respect to my friend who had to find ways to control Purdey's enthusiasm day after day. My friend had not yet managed to find a reliable dog walker for the hours when she was at work, so sometimes the dog would go in to work with her and hang about the staff room or her car, and other times she would be left at home, if someone was able to come and take her out. Probably neither of these options was giving her the exercise she needed in order to drain her energy and be calm.

I gifted my friend some doggie tools to help her continue what I had put in place – various games for her to play when she was left on her own, to alleviate the boredom and stop her chewing anything in sight, and a long training lead, to allow my friend to be able to have control of Purdey at all times, and give a correction if she failed to come back when called.

The importance of the walk on the lead, be it a long or a short lead, is greatly underestimated. This is a time when you are connected to your dog, and the perfect time to show leadership. Your dog should be following your every move. Off lead, the dog is making its own decisions, often the wrong ones. Your dog should think that you are the most interesting thing in the park. The walk is no time to be passive. You need to constantly engage your dog, constantly call him back for rewards or games. Switch off the mobile, and only walk with someone else if you can stay alert to your dog and your surroundings. The walk itself is a primal need for a dog. (Being put out in the garden is no substitute.) In the wild, dogs migrate on a daily basis, following their leader the whole time. This way they feel safe in the knowledge that their leader has everything under control – will lead them to food, water, shelter and ward off enemies. Domestic dogs need to feel the same.

So, I sent Purdey and her owner off with high hopes for a complete rehabilitation.

Some weeks later I bumped into them in the park. Purdey was back to her old self, busy chasing birds, balls, dogs and school children, and my friend was unable to get her to come back. My friend was anxious, as she had already been berated by various parents and dog owners. (Dogs can sense anxiety and will stay away from it. After all, their survival depends on a strong, calm, assertive leader.) She looked guiltily to me for help.

Once she's bolted there's not a lot you could do, I explained. The work you have to put in is before this moment. Like my eyesight, treating the symptom was not the answer. She had to treat the cause. It would be easy enough to stop Purdey running off if we put a lead on her and never let her off, but this would not teach her anything. She would run off again as soon as she was let off the lead. If we looked at *why* she was running off and not coming back, we could change her behaviour for good. She was running off because she did not have an authority figure to answer to, and because my friend had not yet mastered the art of becoming the most interesting thing in the park.

We eventually managed to get Purdey back, by luring her with a squeaky ball and walking *away* from her. As I popped the dog in the back of her car, I saw the training lead sitting on the back seat still in its shiny new packaging.

I completely understand my friend's reasons for doing things her way. But the dog will not change unless the owner is willing to change. I am not attributing blame or judgement. It's just the way things are. I needed to let go of my ego and not assume that everyone needed my advice or wanted to follow it. Firstly, she had never asked me for help. Secondly, she thought that by allowing her agitated dog to run free and have fun, the dog would be happier. Sadly this is a misconception that many dog owners share, fuelled by human psychology, not dog psychology.

It is a fallacy that daily exercise alone makes for a happy dog, even if they are getting masses of it. Understandably, my friend thought that by allowing Purdey to chase birds, the dog was going to be super tired when they got home, and want for nothing else. Yes the dog would be tired, but at what cost? She had had such fun chasing the birds that she was oblivious to her owner's presence and protestations. She came back only when she was ready and not before. Having experienced such fun, the next walk would inevitably be the same, as she would seek to reproduce that 'high'. Ironically, the dog would be getting fitter and fitter and so would be able to chase the birds for longer next time.

Similarly, I often see the same owners out with their dogs clutching one of those ball chuckers. (I have one myself, but use it sparingly). They throw ball after ball for a slightly obsessed dog, and they are delighted because instead of going for a walk they only have to stand there as their dog does all the running. However, if the dogs aren't getting an outlet for their mental energy as well, (sniffing their way around a walk is one way), it simply means that they have more stamina and energy to put into relieving their boredom when at home. Dogs need to sniff, to experience different places, to socialize with different people and other dogs, to solve puzzles, to work and be challenged mentally.

More and more I am seeing unbalanced dogs because they get too much affection, without discipline or enough mental exercise. Just as the most healthy diet (think oily fish, kale and quinoa) does not make a jot of difference if it is not *digested* properly, (ie if you are stressed or eating on the move – believe me I've been there), so the most useful advice is useless if it is not digested properly.

I have learnt to let this one go. Purdey will always be out of control, until some consistent rules are in place.

Or so I thought. Now, in the months that it has taken to write this short book, a wonderful thing has happened.

Having not seen Purdey or her owner for some time, it was lovely to hang out with them for the day recently. We went for a long walk. Purdey was not on the lead. I braced myself for an incident or three. However, she came back when called, and was friendly with every dog we passed. My friend was relaxed and in command. This was obviously having a positive effect on Purdey. She hadn't even brought the ball for the walk, which was her usual crutch to keep the dog from misbehaving. "Well I remember you said she needs to sniff around and just be a dog". She also told me how Purdey loved the mind games they played together. She had escalated from putting the dog's food in a box with the lid on, to putting tape round the box and lid, and letting Purdey figure out how to get in. Genius idea for a dog whose natural tendencies were to chew and dig. Next I suppose she would bury the taped up box!

So she had been listening after all. The rest of her life had just taken precedence for a while. And I was to learn yet again that patience is a virtue.

Mind Games and Mental Stimulation for your Dog

Any dog needs mental, as well as physical stimulation, in order to be balanced and happy. Ten minutes of mental stimulation drains as much energy as a 30 minute walk. Keep it short. We want him to succeed, to boost his confidence, so don't make the task too hard at first. Build up to more complicated games only once he has mastered the easy ones.

There are hundreds of games, but here are a few basic ones to get you started:

1. Give him his meal (if you are feeding kibble-dry dog food in pellet form) in a food dispensing ball, or throw the kibble all over the kitchen floor. He will not be able to gulp his food down, and will have to sniff out all the pieces. It's a good time to walk out and leave him to it.
2. Give him his food in a bowl covered by a tea towel. Progress to a larger towel, and then an upturned cardboard box.

3. Have him sit and watch while you place treats around the room or garden. Tell him to go sniff them out. Make it progressively harder, and start to hide them under cushions etc. This can also be done with a favourite toy.

4. Put a toy/treat in a closed egg box. He will enjoy ripping the box up to get to the treat inside.

5. Place a whole raw egg in its shell on the floor. He will smell the yolk inside and have to figure out how to get in. It's perfectly fine for them to ingest the shell, but maybe not so good for your carpet.

6. Put a treat inside a plastic deli container, with the lid on. He will have to get the lid off to get at the treat. If he walks off or gives up, make it easier and only half secure the lid.

7. Put a treat under an upturned plastic cup. He will smell it and have to knock over the cup in order to get to it. Progress to many cups, but only put treats under a few of them.

8. Fill a muffin tin with tennis balls. (One in each cupcake mould). Put a treat under a few of the balls, and get him to remove the ball to get to the treat.

9. Play hide and seek in the house or garden. Have someone hold him while you go and hide, then call him. Praise him when he finds you. Finding you is reward enough – no treat necessary.

10. Make an obstacle course, or use what nature provides, and get him to jump up onto a tree trunk, and walk along it, then jump over a branch , round a tree, under a bench etc.

11. Teach him a new trick. Ask him to lie down, roll over, high five etc – there's plenty online to guide you through this.

12. Make your games breed appropriate. If you have a terrier, hide something in the ground for him to dig out. If you have a retriever teach him to pick up his toys and bring them to you. If you have a scenthound create a trail for him to follow.

13. Be unpredictable. Always walk a different route. Shake up the routine. Let your dog meet many different people and other dogs, and expose him to different situations and places. And most importantly remember – THE GARDEN IS NO SUBSTITUTE FOR A WALK.

"Soar to the sky of emptiness,
Fly like a swan in flight.
This is the art of mindfulness;
The path is full of light."

BANANI RAY

6

OSCAR: MEDITATION AND FLOW

A day after seeing 'magic' Martin, a little bit of magic *did* happen. It crept in unnoticed. I was walking my dog, and felt more relaxed than usual as I felt I could start to trust what Florina and Martin had told me, and that everything was going to be ok. There had been a shift. My thoughts were absorbed in some music and as I looked around me admiring the trees and the birds, I hardly even noticed that everything was in focus. It was only a while later that I realised I could see perfectly.

I almost didn't dare believe it would last. But I knew I had to believe it, else my own negativity would become the new truth: if I didn't believe it would last, it wouldn't. By the time I reached home, the clarity had faded a bit, but I wasn't too deflated. I had literally seen the possibilities that lay ahead, and the change had happened when I wasn't trying to make a change. I had finally accepted my situation and had **just let things be**.

Sarah was one of the first recipients of my good news. She had been worrying that her worrying would make the cancer come back. She had introduced me to the headspace app, for my anxiety, and I in turn introduced her to Martin for hers. It gave me great satisfaction knowing that one of my more sceptical friends was sold on Martin. To me it meant he really must be the real deal. But we would both find an even stronger lifeline together a few months down the line.

The moments of perfect vision continued to come and go. I was on my way, but there was clearly more work to be done to make this 'surrender to the moment' a daily habit.

I had been thinking about meditation, and its positive effects. Headspace was all the rage and gathering followers. I had read an interesting book by a burnt out newscaster, who had sceptically tried meditation for his recuperation, and even he had reported success. It was honestly, but long windedly titled "10% Happier. How I Tamed the Voice in my Head, Reduced Stress Without Losing my Edge, and Found Self Help that Actually Works".

My first experience of the amazing effects of meditation had actually happened soon after the onset of my weird vision. Going blind had always been my biggest fear since I was a child. My career at the time was all about pleasing the eye, and I have a very visual memory. Where would I be without it? Contemplating blindness set off panic attacks, during which my heart would almost be pounding out of my chest. The attacks happened almost daily at first as I allowed my thoughts to spiral out of control. I went to a doctor who prescribed beta blockers. I never used them (I hate even taking a paracetamol), but they were my safety net.

I had gone to my acupuncturist and warned him my pulse would probably be through the roof, as my heart was pounding so much. On the contrary, he said he could barely feel a pulse at all, so blocked was the energy. He told me to visualise the needle in my head as I lay there, and not to let my thoughts veer away from it. After 30 minutes I was completely calm.

As I was pondering one day, soon after my vision returned, how I could get guidance on meditation and mindfulness, the answer literally landed in my lap.

This seems to happen: the more relaxed and accepting of every moment you are, things just come to you, without having to look for them. Some people call this 'flow'. Walking home that day, I saw a sign outside a chemist shop, advertising courses in mindfulness. I must have walked past this chemist one hundred times and never noticed the sign before. I immediately walked in, and bumped straight into a tower of a woman with flaming curly tresses. This was Shirley, my smiling South African guru.

Shirley is like no other person I have ever met. She exudes positivity. She is non judgemental, lives in the moment, and has a heart the size of her ample bosom. Far from being self righteous, she finds lightness in everything, and I could not conceive, even now, going more than a fortnight without hearing her wise words. She makes me cry, but boy does she make me laugh.

One of my recent clients was suffering from the opposite of 'flow'. She and her dog Oscar, were tragically stuck. Oscar had started to become aggressive: he would bark at strangers and random dogs, and was frenetic in the house, running round, desperate for attention, jumping on furniture and not being told to do otherwise. I started to chat to her to find out when the behaviour started, and she told me that it was shortly after her son had died. He had committed suicide three years previously. Oscar had been his dog. Everything started slotting into place. The dog had been passed around various family members since the son's death, so no-one considered him their dog, and most just felt sorry for him. This is a dangerous emotion; as if you stroke a dog you feel sorry for (a natural human reaction), you are actually nurturing a feeling of insecurity. Insecure dogs often turn to aggression, especially in the absence of any leadership.

Understandably the mother could barely spend time with the dog as he reminded her of her son.

The dog needed leadership, as they all do. But he also had

a role to play in helping the mother heal. Blocking her feelings around the dog was also walling herself up in her deep sadness, blocking all 'flow' and stopping her from living in the present again. We discussed how, instead of feeling sorry for the dog and avoiding him because of the memories he kindled of her son, she might try to feel joy that Oscar gave her a connection to her son, and to allow herself to move on. It was an emotional meeting, and I am no human psychologist, but I knew what was right for the dog. I told her it was ok to feel sad. Allow those thoughts to come and they would pass in their own good time.

You can't stop the waves, but you can learn how to surf.

With her new positive thinking around Oscar's role in her life and with some new leadership skills, she reported just days later that Oscar was a different dog.

The next phase of my life is one I *do* want to remember. It was exciting to have a future ahead of me that was full of positivity, but more importantly it was wonderful to be able to find joy in the present.

Sarah was my mindfulness buddy. We went to see Shirley weekly, and each time we learnt something new and had a shot at meditating. We were the Witches of Chiswick, conjuring up all things good.

Shirley taught us that 98% of our thoughts are useless;

simply don't serve us. Meditation is a way to clear out the brain clutter, if only for a few minutes, and bring you clarity and peace. How many times have you been racking your brain to remember something (say, someone's name), and it's only when you relax those thoughts that the answer comes to you? It comes to you, you don't have to go searching for it.

Making space in the brain calms the thoughts. When trying to cure a dog of aggression, it is important to make space in his brain, so that he does not act impulsively. Merely practising a 'stay' before he gets his food or crosses the road, or gets out of the car, can train his brain to think before he acts. This will lead to him thinking before he lunges at another dog, "Will I get a better reward from attacking this dog, or turning to my master?" You see clarity when the brain is relaxed. It works as well for dogs as it does for humans.

Meditation (being without thought) is a way of helping me be present. I bring my awareness to my breath or the liveliness within my body. If I'm completely still and I put my attention on my hands, I can feel them buzzing and pulsating with the life force within. It's a pretty cool feeling. Often I have my face pulsating at the same time, but try as I might I am yet to perfect feeling any life at all in my feet. There's always more to work on. You might say that surely this exercise involves thought, the one thing we are trying to avoid in this process, but we only need consciousness, not thinking, in order to do this.

When we meditate, we are taking away thoughts. The absence of thought is a wonderful rest for our whirring brains. Ironic then that the word 'thoughtless' has negative connotations, when 'thoughtless' to me is a state of bliss.

Shirley echoed Ekhart Tolle's words about the ego, and I became more conscious of which part of me was the true essence of me, and which was the part trying to impress or judge. When you feel inferior or superior to anyone else, that's your ego talking. Just recognising that is a breakthrough in itself. If I stray from the path, something soon enough will be sent to remind me, and sometimes I need reminding in the most blatantly obvious of ways. During a yoga class recently, I was feeling pretty smug about how my 'utthita hasta padangustasana' was going. (Extended hand to big toe pose, on one leg). Taking a glance around the room, I thought my pose looked in better shape than most. It was at precisely this point that the yoga instructor said, "Leave your ego at the door. Don't worry what your neighbour is doing; just do what feels right for your body". She was clearly talking directly to me.

I learnt from Shirley that the brain has a negativity bias, meaning that if 10 things go right in a day and one thing goes wrong, you will focus on the thing that went wrong. If you put negative thoughts to the back of your mind, and only think about the good stuff, you can actually retrain your brain. Apparently it takes just 17 seconds to create a new neural pathway. So let's say you are walking to work, and you pass an interestingly dressed fellow with a crazy hairdo and a couple of painful looking piercings, instead of thinking, 'did he look in the mirror this morning', or 'those trousers are way too tight', or 'that nose ring makes him look like a bull', you could shift to ' how wonderful that he has the confidence to express himself so uniquely!' Keep that thought in your head for 17 seconds, and bingo, new positive neural pathway.

How often we ask "What's wrong with you?", when we could be asking "What's right with you?" Go to bed summoning up one single positive moment in your day, and you will be surprised how much better you sleep.

In the past I have been very critical, not just to myself in my head, but to people's faces. I wouldn't have hesitated telling a friend that the pattern on their tie looked like they had been sick down it, or the shirt they were wearing looked like a deckchair – I thought that was funny. Sad really. It takes so much more energy to be critical than kind, and offers no rewards. If you are critical of others it generally means you are critical of yourself. I was set the challenge to go a whole day without a single critical thought. Needless to say, I did not succeed, but I did at least recognise when I was being critical, and I could smile to myself about that. Gotcha!

I now smile at a multitude of people I would have normally ignored, and they always smile back, and it makes me happy. Little things, but they make all the difference. Feelings are reflected. If you think better of someone, they'll think better of you. Give what you want to receive.

I found myself softening. The stress hormones triggered by negative emotions such as fear, anger, criticism, intolerance, were becoming more infrequent, and in turn my physical health was improving.

Nature has a way of bringing the most profound joy. A sunset, a spider's web in the frost, a misty morning, birds twittering at dawn, a warm wind on your face – these are easy pleasures. It's less obvious, but equally easy to find joy in mundane things: a hot shower, a delicious meal, a comfy armchair. If you go about your day giving 17 seconds of deliciously benign thought to something, you will be changing your outlook on life, and you *will* be happier. Maybe only 10% happier, but happier nonetheless.

Dogs find this easier than humans. They always live in the moment.

How to Meditate

There are no rules, and many methods. Try some or all of the below. The aim is to empty the mind of thought. If a thought creeps in, which it will, just acknowledge it, let it go, and move back to what you were doing before.

Start with a few minutes only, and gradually increase over time. I find 20 mins is the most I can do without losing it.

Try to make it a daily practice. If you say that you don't have time to meditate once a day, you should probably be doing it twice a day, as you need it the most!

1. Get comfortable. Maybe don't lie down. You might fall asleep. I did.
2. Take some deep cleansing breaths. In through the nose, out through the mouth.
3. Close your eyes.
4. Try and be still.
5. Don't try and block thoughts. Allow yourself to feel whatever is. If thoughts come, acknowledge them and allow them to move on.

6. Scan your body from head to toe, relaxing every muscle as you go, especially in your face. Feel the weight of your body in your seat, and note where the points of contact are.

7. Be aware of the sounds around you. Often I turn to Youtube and put on sounds of waves or rainfall or Tibetan singing bowls, or birdsong etc.

8. Think, "Am I still breathing?" This brings your awareness to your breath. This freaks some people out and then they start to breathe all unnaturally. If that's the case, try a different way.

9. Think, " I wonder what my next thought will be?" This keeps you conscious and alert. The vision of a pointer dog springs to my mind – one paw raised, motionless.

10. Clap your hands once, and see how long the tingle lasts. Eventually you won't need to clap to feel the tingling life force within. Just focus on any part of your body and it will spring to life. Imagine your blood circulating your body. (Unless you are my husband, in which case don't as you will become queasy and probably faint!)

11. Try an open eyes meditation. Stare at a log fire or up through the branches of a tree, or out the window at snow/rain falling.
12. Try a moving meditation. Walk very very slowly and be aware of every muscle moving in your body, the way your clothes rub against you, and the weight of every footstep. Tai chi and qigong are also wonderful moving meditations.
13. Don't be hard on yourself if you can't dispel the thoughts. Some days it's just not happening.

So if happiness was the answer, I created it wherever I could. Nothing changes, without making a change, I reminded myself. Or as Ghandi put it, "Be the change you want to see".

I wanted to find work that would bring me happiness, and would nurture me. In my youth, I fantasised about becoming a vet, as it would give me exposure to the animals I loved. In reality, the 7 years it would take to graduate put me off and my thoughts soon drifted to other careers. Nevertheless I have always felt an affinity with animals, especially dogs, so I thought this natural break in my life the perfect opportunity to try something else new. In my early married life, when living in New York I had mentioned to my husband that I didn't think I was for the rat race, and that all I really wanted to do was look after dogs, and work with them in some capacity. He slightly scoffed at the idea, and rebuffed, I put it to the back of my mind. It wasn't nearly high brow enough for his expectations of me. Well now I was older and wiser, I didn't give a jot for other people's opinions. I've learnt it's so much more important to follow your heart, and be true to yourself.

I volunteered for the summer at Dogs Trust. It wasn't quite what I imagined. Lots of mucking out, washing and feeding; lots of contact with cats, rabbits and mice, but next to none with the dogs. Ask as I might, I was never put on the dog rota, so I left.

It then occurred to me that I should get more involved,

and get trained in something meaty. So this is how I launched myself into the world of canine psychology, and everything became perfectly clear.

I went online and found a course on dog psychology. I enrolled, and was immediately gripped by the programme. There was so much to learn, and hands on experience with the dogs. The last thing on my mind was my vision. The course had my total focus, like a kind of meditation. The less thought I gave my vision, the more I just went with the flow. I was excited about the future, whilst being totally content with the now.

I don't recall any single moment when I realised I could see as well as I used to. No eureka moment. Just a gradual improvement. It had been around six months since that first bleary eyed morning at the front door, and now my vision was completely back to normal. I was not going to take it for granted though. I would keep on the case to increase happiness in my life and stay positive. And yet I couldn't help judging – the medical professionals had been wrong, or had no answer. The alternative and whacky healthcare professionals had been right.

Day one of the psychology course had around 40 applicants squeezed into a village hall. Most had brought their own problematic hounds. We were seated like sardines, with dogs at our feet, trying to make conversation above the chatter and barking and whining. Recipe for disaster I thought – a roomful of screwed up dogs with owners who didn't know how to control them. Then a woman in combats walks in, with purpose, puts two fingers in her mouth, and whistles. The whole room went quiet. She had everyone's attention, humans and dogs alike. She held our attention for an hour and a half until the first break (which she said was for the dogs, not the adults), and there was not a peep out of any of the dogs. If she sensed any dog getting restless she would go over to it and tell it firmly to 'shh' with a click of her fingers, and they abruptly stopped. She stood the entire day – the dogs had to see her as an authority figure, so sitting was not an option.

It's fascinating what you can do with your energy alone. There is a field of frisky horses near our house. My husband and my son cannot walk through it without being set upon by a few bucking and rearing members of the herd. So they run out, with the horses in hot pursuit. I have never encountered this problem, so thought they were exaggerating until I saw it with my own eyes. I realised that because I had no fear of horses, and marched towards them in an assertive way, they sensed no negative energy, and did not need to chase me away.

Calm assertive energy is more powerful than barked commands and physical restraints, we learnt. Combat lady had a very obvious powerful energy, that had humans as well as dogs falling into line. The tutor on the second part of the course was more softly spoken, and I made the mistake of pre-judging her, thinking she could never command a pack of dogs with her gentle approach. But she transformed into supergirl in the presence of her pack. Calm but firm. And the dogs lapped it up and were eager for more instruction.

It's interesting to know that dogs in the wild will chase off any dog showing weak energy. The pack's survival depends on it. If your dog is fearful or anxious you may find it gets set upon by other dogs when out walking, and this is why. The only cure is to build up your dog's confidence.

I returned home from the psychology course eager to test what I had learned on my own dog. She is a docile old lab, bless her, but annoyingly slow walking down the street. She would stop and sniff and pee so often it took forever to get to the park. I took her out this time with a new train of thought – 'there will be no stopping today'. I was ready to give a correction on the lead the first time she stopped, but miraculously she didn't stop once. She just sensed my new energy – read my mind almost – and stepped into line. I hadn't uttered a word . This stuff really worked!

A change in me, brought about a change in her. And this is what I now tell my clients; their dogs will not change, until they themselves change. Essentially I am not training the dog at all – just the owner.

Just as **your thoughts become your reality**, so I tell my clients to make their thoughts their reality. If they don't believe it will work, it generally doesn't. Dogs can sense this.

Now if I am advocating to become more like a dog, I mean a balanced dog. One with no behavioural issues. One without stress, who doesn't bark excessively, or chase his tail, or who is fearful or aggressive. Balanced dogs just have what it is to be happy.

After the dog psychology course, I was sent off to complete 100 case studies before I could graduate. I advertised my services as being free on a local website and was inundated by requests. It was a huge learning curve for me, as you can see by some of the cases I have highlighted. On my quest to do something meaningful which made me happy, I set out to bring back equilibrium to the lives of as many dogs as I could, which in turn might enable their owners to see the beauty of what they could learn from their furry friends.

I've now treated several hundred animals (and their owners). I think that if I had not been on the health journey I had, then I would not have had such an affinity with dog psychology. Not only had I a deeper understanding of the power of energy and positive thinking, but I realised the many parallels of training your mind and training a dog.

I would never consider trying to learn something new if my mind was anxious or in turmoil, now. The stress would take over and my concentration would be thin. Similarly, I cannot expect a dog to learn a new way of being until he is calm. Only then will I have his attention. This is how I begin.

I do believe that there is a new calmness in me that was pushed to one side for years and years, in favour of rushing to get a job done, stressing that I wouldn't be good enough, and cramming as much as I could into a short space of time. I felt that was 'achieving'. But now I realise that I achieve much more when I am calm. I will not let myself get worked up if I am late for a meeting. I'll just tell them I'll be late – the world's not going to end. I'm a terrible flyer but I can just about handle turbulence on a plane these days by remaining calm and being in the moment, not catastrophising that the world *is* going to end. I save myself so much unnecessary worry and wasted energy. I even drive at the speed limit now – if you've ever been in a car with me you'll know what a small miracle this is! and I no longer get stressed in traffic jams. If I surrender to the moment and stop resisting, things become much more manageable. This is what dogs do – surrender to the moment. I was already learning to be more dog.

The Benefits of Meditation

Yet ironically, the goal of meditation is no goal. It is simply to be present.

- Lower blood pressure
- Improved blood circulation
- Lower heart rate
- Less perspiration
- Slower respiratory rate
- Less anxiety
- Lower blood cortisol levels
- More feelings of well-being
- Less stress
- Deeper relaxation
- Calm mind
- Lengthened attention span
- Improved sleep

"Try not to become a man of success. Rather become a man of value."

ALBERT EINSTEIN

7

PLATO, STAN & OLLIE: LIVE IN THE MOMENT

Just be. This was the message I kept hearing in the months of my recovery. Not thinking of the past or the future, but just sitting like a dog, enjoying the moment. Although the future had been worrying me, it wasn't until I overcame this worry that my eyesight returned.

Dogs do not have this affliction of fretting about the future. It would be such a blessing if we could be more like them and let go of past and future anxieties.

When one of my girlfriends went on holiday, she booked her dog walker to have her two dogs Stan and Ollie for the week. She left for the airport early and made arrangements for the dog walker to pick up the dogs later that morning. Returning refreshed after a week's break, she and her daughter were excited to see the dogs again, so they were thrilled when they opened the front door and could hear from the barking coming from the kitchen that they had already been returned. She opened the kitchen door and one dog limped towards her and the other lay wagging its tail gently in its basket. She looked around at the curtains still closed as she had left them, and at the week's supply of dog food still sitting for collection along with a present for the dog walker, on the counter. With horror the realisation hit her: these poor dogs had never left the kitchen. They had been on their own with no food or water all the 8 days she had been away. The only saving grace had been that my friend had forgotten to lock the dog flap, so they had been able to go outside to relieve themselves, and lick up any rain water.

She immediately rang the dog walker. With no apology he explained that he had had a stressful week and that it had slipped his mind!

When she recounted this story to me, I immediately wanted to bad mouth the dog walker. But she blamed herself, and you can imagine how guilt ridden she felt. I had to explain that the dogs had already moved on mentally and so must she. They were happy to see her, they recovered, they hold no grudges. If she had held on to guilt, it would have affected her behaviour towards them (by spoiling them and allowing them to do things that were not usually permitted) which in turn might have actually *created* behavioural problems. I urged her to carry on as normal and do as her dogs had done. Forget the past.

I don't suppose dogs have many thoughts in a day. They are certainly not thinking "I wonder what's for supper tonight?" or "How am I going to punish my owner for leaving me alone for so long?". They just roll with life, not obsessing about the past or worrying about the future, and see how happy they are.

A case I took on some months later demonstrates how quickly a dog can change, if the owner is willing to let go of the past.

Plato, a black labrador, was one of my first real cases, and by real I mean someone actually sought me out and asked for my services. My first paying customer. I didn't have to rely on friends and family any more. Plato's owner was an intelligent child psychologist. Her young clients would come to her house for therapy and Plato would sit in the consulting room and be on hand if there were any tears. Although she was doing right by the children, using Plato to soothe away the pain, she did not realise that Plato was absorbing so much negative energy which was stressful for him. He felt everyone around him was weak and therefore he had to take up the reins of being leader and protector. Quite a weight to bear when you are exposed to this every single day. At least the owner understood that when outside the house her negative energy was fuelling her dog's behaviour. The lady had been bitten by a dog as a child, and since then was convinced that any large or bullish looking dog was going to attack her. Plato, sensing her fear, would try and protect her by lashing out at any dogs that passed. She told me that just the day before, she had been walking in the park when she saw a rottweiler off lead. She then rushed, pulling Plato, to the security of the enclosed dog area, until the rottweiler was out of sight. How emotionally fuelled were these walks for her and Plato. I didn't know who I felt more sorry for.

Plato was a sweetheart in the house – polite and obedient, but as soon as his owner starting donning her coat and getting the lead, the whole mood changed. I could see the tension on her face as she clipped the lead onto a now excited Plato. She wrapped the lead 3 times around her hand, making the dog feel tense, and tentatively looked up and down the street for any signs of 'danger'. (I actually had to stop her here, and we went back inside to learn how to exit the house in a calm manner.)

The owner was on high alert as we walked down the street. I told her I was going to fetch my lab from the car, to act as a calming influence on Plato, and she nearly had a panic attack, "oh no, what if Plato attacks your dog!". I asked her to let go of the lead and hang back for the introduction, as her tension was sending all the wrong signals down the lead to her dog. Of course the meeting was fine, as I knew it would be, and after that we enjoyed a leisurely walk together and she relaxed. Plato, sensing a new security, did not react to any of the dogs we passed. The owner actually cried, not just with relief, but with happiness for her dog who was enjoying his first walk outside in years. The tears were also tinged with sadness that she had prevented Plato from just being a normal happy dog for so long.

Plato's owner has been working on her confidence around other dogs, helped by now being able to read their body language. If they are relaxed, she is relaxed. I recommended to keep Plato out of the consulting room, and to only use him as a 'reward' for the children after their therapy session, so as to be able to end on a happy note. He has reacted well to this new positive energy, and continues to improve.

Plato never got up in the morning and thought "Who shall I attack today?". It was his owner who thought "Who is Plato going to attack today?". Her anticipation had fuelled her dog's behaviour in that moment.

All dogs merely react to each circumstance as it happens, governed by whatever energy surrounds them. Plato's owner was living in fear of what had happened in the past, and couldn't let go of it. She let it affect her present and her future. When dogs leave the house, they don't know if they are leaving for 5 minutes or for a week, and they just go with the flow. A perfect example of living in the present. We have a lot to learn from them.

Just trust in the process of life.

This is easier said than done. It's not second nature to sit back and trust that life will just happen, without striving to mould it and make it happen. It is a very hard thing to unlearn values you have been taught, by teachers, family and society in general – values such as, "To be successful, you have to strive hard and make lots of money", "We must not be selfish", "When you've made up your mind, stick with it, don't be flaky". But this was exactly what I was trying to do – to unlearn. These are only beliefs, and if we change what we believe in then we can set ourselves free.

Depak Chopra, a prominent spiritual teacher, teaches that 'beliefs create reality'. The brain is a powerful tool which alters your behaviour based on what you believe to be true. The most obvious example of this is the placebo effect. (Patients are cured by a sugar pill because they are told it will make them better, and they *believe* it.)

It's easy to change our belief systems from negative to positive. It's a wholly good thing to be selfish – to love yourself and be kind to yourself. Put yourself first, and then you will be in a healthy place to be able to help others. Change your mind as often as you want – there will be good reasons for it. Follow your heart. **Success should be measured by how much joy you have in a day**, not by the car you drive or the house you live in.

Maya Angelou teaches that success is 'liking yourself, liking what you do, and liking how you do it'.

"The purpose of our lives is to be happy", according to the Dalai Lama, not to be successful. When he was asked what most surprised him about humanity , he replied:

"Man. Because he sacrifices his health in order to make money. Then he sacrifices his money to recuperate his health. And then he is so anxious about the future that he doesn't enjoy the present: the result being that he doesn't live in the present or the future. He lives as if he is never going to die, and then dies having never really lived".

If we learn to live in the moment and be more present, we can get off that treadmill.

Eckhart Tolle tells a story in his book "A New Earth" which demonstrates the reluctance of the human mind to let go of the past: A group of monks were walking in silent contemplation, when they came across a young lady in a kimono stranded one side of a muddy puddle . Not wishing her any distress about getting her shoes and dress ruined, one of the monks went over to her and offered her his hand, and lifted her safely over the puddle. Some hours later when they arrived back into the seclusion of the monastery, a second monk said to the first, "You should not have carried her over the puddle; it is not seemly for men in our position to be touching women". "I see you are still carrying her", the first monk replied. "I put her down 3 hours ago".

We get weighed down by negative feelings, and the brain keeps them alive by obsessing over them. It is second nature to hold on to the past and it takes some mind training to be any other way, unless you have a natural aptitude for it.

I have to keep learning this.

My daughter and my niece are best friends. They are very similar, yet very different. My daughter loves a party – loves to dance, socialise, listen to music and not take life too seriously. She makes people happy. My niece has all of these attributes too, but has her head screwed on a little more.

My older sister asked my daughter over lunch what she would like to do in the future.

"I don't know. Have fun. Go to festivals".

"But what exactly is it about festivals you like?", she guided (she is a teacher after all).

"Do you want to maybe work at one or perform in one, one day?"

"Er, I dunno really. I haven't thought that far ahead. I just want to have fun."

I shrunk into my chair and cringed inside. My niece had just told us how she had plans to work at a local opera and do charity work abroad for a turtle conservation in her year off, before going to university – and she is a year younger than my daughter, not yet even completed her A levels. Every mother wants to be proud of their offspring, and at that point in time it would be an understatement to say I wasn't feeling it!

I went with these thoughts the following week to Shirley.

"How wonderful she sounds," she said. " She is a master of living in the moment".

And bit by bit she turned it around for me. My girl was *already* a success, as she found fun and laughter in everything day after day. She would fall on her feet as she was such a free spirit. My concern did not come from a place of love, but a place of fear. It was my fear that was driving my negative thoughts. Fear that she might fail if she didn't plan ahead. She had no such fears. I have so much to learn from her. She was showing me a little bit of heaven on earth. She is definitely 'more dog' than most. No planning, no worrying, just flying by the seat of her pants! With confidence.

My daughter and my husband are very alike in this respect. Easy-going, 'go with the flow' people pleasers. It used to annoy me how his best advice to me about any problem would be 'just get over it'. But I see now how liberating that is. Accept the situation and move on. Like dogs.

He has been very long suffering, watching my meta-morphosis over the last few years. He used to sadly say, "You're not the girl I married", but now I think he's thankful that I am not. I certainly am. And where once I wondered if our diverging paths would be our demise, I now believe conversely that they have brought us closer together.

How to be Present

You can only access happiness in the present, so it's really worth practising.

Presence is awareness. I find if you get still, you can get there easily.

1. Meditate. This brings immediate awareness to your body and surroundings.
2. Turn to nature. Enjoy a sunrise, the delicacy of a flower's petals, the heat of the sun on your skin, the sound of crickets in the grass, a field of corn swaying in the wind etc. Appreciate the structure and majesty of a tree, without naming it a tree.
3. Be aware of your senses. Really feel the water bouncing off your skin during your morning shower, and enjoy its heat. Most people are already mentally in the office when they do this, and the enjoyment of the present moment is wasted. Eat mindfully. Savour each mouthful of that croissant. Listen to the birds singing on your walk to the train station or to that incredible instrumental Pink Floyd track on your air pods. Look at each raindrop as it collects and falls down the window pane. Savour the

smell of your macchiato before you drink it.

4. Do some physical or creative activity. The concentration needed to perform will keep your thoughts from wandering.

5. Go within. Focus on your breath and the life force within your veins. Do a body scan.

6. Say "Fuck it" more often. Release the past and surrender to what is.

7. Step away from the digital world. Turn off all devices and just take a look around you.

8. Be more like your dog. Don't hold grudges. Forgive.

"Dogs do speak, but only to those who know how to listen."

ORHAN PAMUK

8

OTTO:
MISUNDERSTANDING

Your dog spends all day reading your body language, so it's only fair we should spend some time reading his, if you are to have a healthy and happy two way relationship. If we misinterpret his behaviour it can have disastrous consequences. He can be encouraged or intimidated by changes in your posture or facial expression. He is also influenced by your tone of voice. High pitched squawking will over excite him, whilst deep tones and shouting will scare him. It's unlikely he'll follow either.

One of the saddest cases I have been called in to help with was at the home of a lovely couple, who were having trouble with their schnoodle (schnauzer/poodle). They told me he had a habit of pooing in the house out of revenge. He had even pooed on their bed. (He was 3 years old and perfectly house trained.) "Revenge for what?" I asked. "For leaving him on his own in the house," they replied. This was not his only problem. He was also very destructive. He had completely shredded the stair carpet which they had had to replace, and so now they kept him locked in a small room when they went out, to avoid further mishaps. I asked to see the room. It had glazed doors onto the garden, but no access to it, and a door onto the kitchen which was scratched to pieces. A distressing sign.

I asked how they reacted when they came home to find dog mess. "Well we beat him of course to teach him that it's bad behaviour." And yet here he was looking up lovingly at them.

This poor dog! Devoted and faithful companion, not knowing what he was doing to get shouted at and beaten. How could he associate the beating with the poo when there was such a time lapse between them? It was achingly obvious that he was not only bored and frustrated when left alone, but stressed and anxious too. He was only taken out the house for short periods once or twice a day, and was left on his own with nothing to do for long periods of time.

I explained that dogs do not rationalise. They are not vengeful. They live in the moment. I had to explain that the poo on the bed should actually be viewed as flattery, as Otto in his stress was seeking out a place he felt safe, and smelt of them. I tried to help them see it from Otto's point of view. On his own for hours and without having had a walk, he would have loads of pent up mental and physical energy. With nothing to do or toys to play with he would be bored and stressed. Chewing helps alleviate stress in dogs so he chewed whatever he could find. Locked in the room off the kitchen, no wonder he had scratched the door trying to get out, as he would have been looking for something to chew, something to do, somewhere safe to go. As the owners walked in the door at the end of the day, he would be anticipating getting shouted at. Not because of the poo but because that's what they always did when they got home. He would cower – dog body language to stop hostility – and it would be read as guilt. (If he were an aggressive dog he might growl to defend himself, if he were a clever dog he would realise that humans had a weird thing for poo because they always rubbed his nose in it, and so he might eat it to stop that happening!) He would get beaten and shouted at and get stressed out all over again. Was it any wonder therefore that when the owners took the dog outside that he didn't perform in front of them, knowing their fixation with poo. He would wait until they left the house and then do it in the corner of a room where they wouldn't find it.

Nothing changes without making a change, remember. This cycle had to stop and the owners, deeply saddened by what they had unwittingly created, did make lots of changes, and there have been no more incidents.

Once owners understand their dog/human relationship from the dog's point of view, their life together is a more harmonious one.

How to Read your Dog's Body Language

Your dog is continuously giving you (and other dogs) signals of how he is feeling. If you know what your dog is 'saying' you will be able to have a more harmonious relationship.

Tail docking and dressing dogs in clothes can lead to your dog being misread by another dog, as it hides the subtleties of their body language. Similarly, humans can inadvertently put their dogs into a position where they are misread. For example, by pulling up on the lead when they meet another aggressive looking dog, they are actually putting the dog into an aggressive stance. This posture, coupled with the tension on the lead will almost certainly make the situation worse.

There are a myriad of subtle postures, but here are some of the easier ones to read.

- Hackles up. Not aggressive as most people think. Just means your dog is unsure.
- Wagging tail. Doesn't always mean your dog is happy. Can also be a sign of arousal or frustration.
- Tail held high. Confident or aroused. In dominant unneutered males, this can be enough to start a fight.
- Tail held very low or between the legs. Lack of confidence. Nervous.
- Tail held midway, 'wavy' body. Relaxed.
- Lowering the body, ears back, lowering the head, lip licking, taking a wide curved route around another dog, turning the head away from another dog, rolling onto back to expose belly. Appeasement.
- Cowering. Not guilt! Fear in the face of a threat.
- Whale eyes. Showing the whites of their eyes, and looking up from a lowered position. Fear and anxiety.
- Body freeze. Watch out as this can precede a reaction (fight or flight).
- Stiff body, ears forward, eyes locked onto another dog, walking in a straight line towards that dog, head high , tail up, meet face to face. Super confident, and can be

perceived as threatening by another dog, so be alert.

- Panting, when not out of breath or hot. Stressed.
- Shaking. Not always fear. It's the release of adrenaline as he goes from one state of mind into another.
- Closed mouth. Be alert. Your dog is sizing up the situation ready for action.
- Shaking bodies as they would to shake off water. Releasing stress and tension. Going from one state of mind into another.
- Growling, air snapping. Last warning before he bites.
- Bite and hold. Intent to harm.

Be aware of your dog's energy in context to his body language, so you are not confused by the double meaning of some signals. Ears back may be signaling calm submission, if he is trotting along nicely beside you, but it may also mean he is afraid, if his tail is between his legs. A dog who puts his forearms on another dog's back could be displaying dominant tendencies, or it could just be in play.

I was once as in the dark as Otto's owners. I misunderstood my dog's behaviour, and felt so guilty afterwards. I had a rule that she was not allowed on the furniture, but instead I gave her the most comfortable beanbag to lie on. On the odd occasion I would come down in the morning and find her on the sofa in the kitchen where she had been locked up for the night. I would sternly reprimand her and pull her off. She would leave a pile of white hair all over the upholstery, and it drove me nuts. I thought she moulted an insane amount for a labrador. The moulting was inexplicably worse in the winter than the summer. Her hair would get blown like tumbleweed into bundles all over the kitchen floor, and even daily hoovering could not contain it. Neither could I understand why she continued to get on the sofa night after night, having had a telling off, "naughty, bad dog". It got to the point where I would come down in the morning and open the kitchen door, and whether she was on the sofa or not, she would be cowering at my appearance, anticipating a telling off. I misread her expression as guilt. I am ashamed to admit that I even resorted to buying a 'scat mat' online, which I intended to leave on the sofa over night. A scat mat is a plastic mat about the size of 2 doormats, and it has an electric charge running through it, powered by a battery. There was only one setting. I thought it only fair to test it on myself first and I almost jumped out of my skin. It was a serious shock. I am glad to say I did not use it after that, and resorted to laying books all along the sofa instead.

Regrettably, it was only years later that I figured it all out. She was not being naughty at all. She was merely acting in the moment. She got too hot on her beanbag on the underfloor heating, and had to get up off the floor, for she couldn't leave the room to the coolness of the hall. This also explained the excessive moulting. She now sleeps in another cooler room. It's only now that I know dogs are not naughty for the hell of it. There is purpose and meaning in everything they do. It is their survival mechanism.

So every time I see unwanted behaviour in my dog, I question **what have *I* done to create that behaviour.** Dogs were perfect before humans came into the equation.

Way too often, instead of trying to be more dog, we make the mistake of trying to make our dogs more like us. We imagine them as our baby, our child, our spouse, our best friend. We dress them up in clothes, feed them fancy dog food out of personalised bowls, allow them to sit on the furniture and watch television with us, sleep with them in our beds. We give them a boxful of toys and the run of the house and garden thinking they could want for nothing, but even a palace will not make a dog happy unless he has regular mental and physical exercise, a calm assertive understanding owner, and rules and boundaries. We have misunderstood what they need. Whilst giving them everything we think they need, we are actually giving them everything that we humans need, and we forget that they are animals, and by doing that we unwittingly create the behaviours we least want. Ironically, by giving them everything to make them the perfect happy pet, we make monsters of them.

It's a natural human desire to want to cuddle and show affection to a dog, but if this is all the dog is getting, then this is actually a form of neglect. You wouldn't raise a child on affection alone. The child needs discipline and rules in order to grow and learn. The child also needs new experiences, a guiding hand, exercise and a purpose (going to school, learning, achieving, and growing mentally). Dogs need the same. But the difference is, you are not going to hurt your dog's feelings if you do not give it affection.

We must be our dog's guardian and decision maker, and give them a purpose. They are not toys to be played with when we feel the need. A dog needs to know that someone is in charge. That someone should not negotiate. The leader decides, and the rest follow. Simple. Zero tolerance. That is what works for dogs and herds of animals in the wild. They show no behavioural problems.

We expect dogs to be able to rationalise, and to understand when they can and can't do things. It's no good allowing your dog to sleep on your bed and then getting cross at him for jumping up there after a muddy walk. He does not know the sheets have just been changed or that he is muddy. He will get stressed, unsure of what he can or cannot do. Make the rules, and stick to them, for your dog's sake.

By taking dogs into our homes and domesticating them, we have effectively taken away their 'freedom'. We therefore have a responsibility to fulfil their natural animal needs if we want them to be happy and problem free.

Recipe for Disaster

There are some common misconceptions out there about how we can treat dogs, and I'd like to dispel a few myths.

Here are some of the biggest no-nos, which can lead to behavioural problems:

- **Weigh** up how many rules you want to set, and decide on none because rules are mean, right?

- **Pour** your heart out to your dog, and cry into his fur.

- **Mix** in a little leniency and ignore his strange obsessions – they're kind of cute!

- **Add** a large dose of affection to an anxious dog.

- **Wrap** the lead tightly around your hand.

- **Grill** him when he's been naughty. "What have you done?" He knows he's done wrong as he looks guilty.

- **Turn up the heat**. Shout at your dog as it's the only way they'll listen. Punish for bad behaviour.

- **Set aside to rest**. Leave your dog on his own for long periods of time with nothing to do, they're just dogs after all.

- **Leave to cool**. Put your dog in the garden then you won't need to walk him.

*"The world would be a nicer place
if everyone had the ability to
love unconditionally as a dog."*

M.K. CLINTON

9

CHARLIE: MOVING FORWARD

I continued to learn something about my own life from almost every dog that I saw, and Charlie was no exception. She was an eight year old wiry terrier/Irish wolf hound cross, with the sweetest temperament, but due to being exposed to fireworks in her youth, she was very jumpy about loud noises, and refused to even go out of the house if it was dark. The poor animal had been fearful like this for the last five years, and her behaviour was quite ingrained. It was going to take time to undo. Being on the top floor flat with no outdoor space, it was a little tricky in winter to get Charlie to go for a pee outside before bedtime. I asked the owners to show me the usual evening routine. The husband went up to her on her bed and clipped the lead on. He said in a firm, no nonsense way, "come on, up you get, out". Normally I would encourage this way of talking, with no fussing – it's what a leader would do – but Charlie needed a softer approach. She began lip licking – a sign of appeasement – she really didn't want to displease her master, but she was a little scared. The husband began to pull her off her bed by the lead, but her collar just came off her head, and she cowered back down. I stopped it there – she was clearly stressed and wasn't going anywhere like this.

It's important in situations like this that the dog comes to you, not you approach the dog. They need to come because they are willing, not because they are being forced. If you pull a dog, they will automatically pull against you. It also creates tension down the lead, and as the handler gets more stressed, so does the dog.

I waved some smoky bacon under Charlie's nose and walked away. She came to me and I put the lead on. Then we played a couple of games for bacon rewards, then I cheerfully said "come on", and headed for the door. She did put the breaks on for a second, but I slackened the lead after only one short sharp tug. She had to come of her own accord. And she did. All the way down 3 flights of stairs and outside to more exciting games and treats. The owners have done an amazing job with her since then, and really put in the hours to bring about a positive change.

The analogy to this story presented itself a week later. My son was studying for his GCSEs. I had tried to drop the tiger mum act since becoming a little more self aware, but I still felt that a certain amount of whip cracking was necessary to get his face off his double screening and into a book.

"You have your French Oral soon and you should be doing at least 2 hours revision today".

Grunt, grunt. Mumble. Possibly a bit of swearing. And off he went out!

Some days later I changed tack. What if I took the same approach I had done with Charlie. If I slackened my grip, would he come voluntarily? I told him that he was an adult now and responsible for his own future. I was going to stop the nagging. He could do as much or as little revision as he saw fit. His future was in his hands.

The following week I received a text from him, which read,

"K also im gunna regret
saying this but you need
to force me to do at least
4 hrs wk on the weekend".

And so I trundled along. Case after case. Confidence growing. I felt good.

I was feeling physically strong too. I slowly slipped back into my old routine of 'doing'. Achieve, improve, achieve, improve. Days were filled with assignments for my design company, for I was back at work now, and evenings after work were filled with a crazy schedule of hobbies – Monday was fencing, Wednesday tae bo, Thursday gospel, Friday tennis, Saturday yoga, Sunday rest day – well, gardening, cooking, entertaining… Which left me Tuesdays to go out if I had any energy left. All the while I was still trying to fit in dog psychology cases and walking my own dog twice a day. With all this striving to improve myself, when was I ever going to 'arrive' and be good enough?

One Sunday I had a fencing competition. These tended to go on most of the day, and were always on Sundays so I didn't do that many of them. My team and I had been trophy winners in the past, so I was ready for another dopamine hit.

Around half way through the day, I was chatting strategies to my team-mates. As I was querying how to counter attack a particularly aggressive player, my vision did something I'd not experienced before. It seemed like a corner of my sight was pixilated and bright. Instead of going into my old default panic position, I took a pause and a breath, made my excuses and walked away. It had been over a year since my sight had fully recovered, so this felt like a scary blast from the past. I thought maybe the fluorescent lighting in the hall was affecting me, so I went outside. To my dismay, it was just as bad outside as it was in. I could feel panic rising up inside me and tried to stifle it. I didn't tell anyone of my predicament, as didn't want any fuss. I had about half an hour until my next fight, so had to make up my mind whether to walk or carry on. I then had the forethought to book an appointment with Magic Martin. He was normally busy for 6 weeks in advance, but maybe there might be a cancellation. Even though it was Sunday, the health shop he worked in was open, and someone answered the phone. Against all odds, there was a free spot the following morning. I can't tell you what relief that brought me. So much so that a few minutes after I came off the phone, the pixilation had completely gone.

I went to the appointment anyway. He told me I had been putting too much pressure on myself to 'do' things and succeed. I was like one of those performers spinning plate after plate after plate. Sooner or later one of those plates was going to have to fall, as I couldn't keep them all spinning, there were just too many of them. Why did I need to achieve so much? Still desperate to try and please my father. (Another old habit, stretching back to my school days.) I had to love and accept myself for who I was today, not for who I might become.

I gave up competitive fencing from then on. I still go training once a fortnight, but just for pleasure. It wasn't just the fencing of course that had to give – it was everything. Everything had to be in moderation. And when I start to exceed moderation, or I get stressed, my left eye twitches to tell me to slow down, and I thank it, and listen.

Sometimes the only way forward is to just be where you are.

"By just spending a few minutes in gratitude each day, you'll notice your thoughts start to shift... You'll also notice your mood shifting. You'll feel better. Joyous, even. And when you're in that joyous, happy place – that's when the miracles start happening."

JOSIE ROBINSON

❿
WILLA: ACCEPTANCE

Thoughts are clever little buggers! They can lead us spiralling down a dark hole, or they can lift us soaring up into the heavens.

But we forget that we can choose our thoughts. How wonderful. **What we focus on grows. What we resist persists.**

All that focusing on my 'illness', or whatever I should call it, and how to get better, was probably why it took me so long to come out the other end. Instead, I should have been focusing on day to day happiness. Not fighting what IS. When we obsess about a feeling, we keep it locked in place, instead of accepting it and allowing it to pass of its own accord. I'm reminded of an anecdote Shirley told me about a wise man who fell off the top of a waterfall into the turbulent water below. People who saw him fall were certain he could not survive, so were astonished when they saw him climb out the river downstream. "How did you do that?" they asked. "I didn't fight it. I became one with the water," he replied.

A friend of mine recently worded the same thing rather differently: "If you lock your dog and your wife in the car, which one will be smiling at you when you return 2 hours later?"

Eckhart Tolle teaches not to fight with what is. We have 3 logical choices: to change what is; to leave what is; to accept what is.

Similarly, Cesar Millan, the dog whisperer, teaches that dogs have 3 logical choices: fight; flight/avoid; surrender. Surrender being the one we want to instill. It's only when they surrender to a situation that balance is restored. And it's the same for us. For instance, if a dog refuses to get into a car – and I have had one of these cases – he can fight against it by throwing a tantrum or biting, but the same thing will happen next time, or he can try and run away, but he will be fetched and brought back to the car again, or he can surrender, and get in the car (not by force), and the problem will not present itself again.

How can we move forward until we have fully accepted and digested the current situation we find ourselves in? Don't fight what is. Be what you already are. Without acceptance there is a feeling of brushing things under the carpet, only to be found at a later date, and then you have to deal with them all over again.

Impressed with how far I had come in the world of dog psychology, and seeing that it was clearly not a fad, but a true commitment, my husband took me out to dinner to propose something. He works in television and could see the possibility of his company backing me to make a tv show about me. His idea was that each week would focus on a couple of unruly/screwed up dogs and their owners, and how I changed their lives around by 'fixing' their dogs. Although there has been a similar show in the UK recently, it didn't get much recognition, and certainly didn't have a middle aged female interior designer at the helm.

I had mixed feelings about his idea. I was delighted and chuffed that he wanted to support me in this way, and that he obviously felt I was on to something worthy. However, he was coming at it from his perspective. I do not share his ambition and drive to always take things further. If you are always striving to achieve more, then when do you get there? When can you call yourself a success? I am very happy where I am right now, and I'd like to stay here and enjoy it some more. Content in the present and not fretting about the future. The thought of being filmed and put on tv scares me somewhat. But who knows – watch this space.

I do believe that it's no coincidence we get the dogs we need, rather than the dogs we want. It's curious how things work out that way. My dear old lab Willa is now very slow, and where we were once matched in high levels of energy, she is now lacking, and I have to remind myself as I pause and wait for her every few minutes when out on a walk, that she is 84 in human years. But the beauty of it is that she has unwittingly made me slow down. I have finally accepted it. Walks have to be shorter and slower, and I no longer tug at her to speed up. And the walks are much more enjoyable now I have surrendered to the situation. She is giving me exactly what I need in my life right now. She is teaching me patience and understanding, whilst reminding me to take it easy. She is also now almost completely deaf. I cannot raise my voice to call her, for she cannot hear. I have to rely on my calm assertive energy and my body language to pull her into line. I have found that adopting this method in other areas of my life has had a great effect too. My children respond so much better to me when I do not raise my voice. My dog has taught me that without uttering a word. What's your dog teaching you?

Willa, like most dogs, is a master of acceptance. She has accepted her lot in life. She has been dealt a mixed hand. Having been given to a rehoming centre when she was only 6 months old, I feel that she has been lucky in being adopted by me (and vice versa). Yet for most of her adult life she has lived with the pain of arthritis. A recent trip to the vet revealed on presentation of her x-rays, that she was riddled with the disease, and he was surprised that she was still walking, let alone jumping in and out of the car. She had never whined or complained. Never let me know the extent of her condition. She did not 'become' her illness, as so many humans would have done. This is largely why, when this book is finished, I will no longer go back in time and think about my 'illness' that was, or define myself by it. My weakened state may have been triggered by my daughter moving out of home, but it was in fact the making of me. And it's that new me which I will focus on. The old book will be closed.

Our dogs are continually teaching us something. How to accept, how to forgive, how to be wildly happy over the smallest things, how to sleep peacefully without worrying about what the next day might bring, how to go with the flow and how to love unconditionally. If mankind could live like dogs, in the moment, there would be no grudges, no revenge, no war, and the world would be a happier place.

Looking back, I can recognise the episode that surrounded the problem with my eyes as my mid life crisis. My vision is perfect now. (At least as perfect as it was before all this began). But maybe the thing that I failed to see then, is that I was already perfect just the way I was. Maybe my sight had to be partially taken away from me to be able to see what was right in front of me. I didn't have to strive to improve myself, to be the best I could possibly be. I just had to enjoy who I was. I didn't have to worry about the future, or regret the past. I had to stop looking for the answer. Maybe there was no answer. Maybe I already had the answer, but couldn't see it.

Could I allow things to be just as they are, like dogs? I am still learning to do this.

Just yesterday, I was in the waiting room at the vet's. A woman came in with a young husky type. The dog was still a puppy and rather beautiful in his fluffy whiteness with blue eyes, and you could tell the lady owner was very proud to be the envy of all eyes in the room. The husky started to bark at a cat in its carrier. The owner did nothing. There's me thinking "correction needed!" The dog continued to bark, and eventually the owner gently said "shh" and stroked him.

In my head: "She's just praised him for barking at the cat!" No wonder then that he soon started up again.

At this point the receptionist behind the desk got involved and called the dog over and gave him a treat to try and distract him.

"OMG, another reward for his bad conduct!"

It was blindingly obvious to me that they were unwittingly making this dog into a cat chaser. I was itching to step in and say something. Did they ask for my help? Would they be thankful for the advice? Probably not. I would just be an interfering old busy body know it all. Could I allow things to be just as they are? Yes, but with difficulty!

How to Build a Great Relationship with your Dog

- Be your dog's pack leader
- Set rules and healthy boundaries, and be consistent about keeping them
- It's never too soon or too late to start training your dog. You can teach an old dog new tricks
- Give your dog a purpose. Take his breed and characteristics into account when finding an outlet for his energy and natural instincts
- Walk with your dog at least twice a day (40 mins each walk). Don't always take the same route. Be unpredictable and keep him interested
- Mentally stimulate your dog. Play mind games and puzzles. Teach him a new trick
- Expose your dog to being away from you when he is young, so he does not develop a dependency or separation anxiety. But never leave any dog on their own for more than 4 hours
- Learn about his body language, so you know what he's 'saying'
- Don't use punishment. It doesn't work. It doesn't get your dog to follow you, and can often exacerbate the situation

- Give affection at the right time. If you show affection to a scared, excited or aggressive dog, you are nurturing that state of mind. Its like saying, "Well done, this is how I want you to be". Give affection when your dog is calm
- Ask your vet about the pros and cons of neutering if you don't want to breed from your dog . Some behavioural problems can be hormone based
- Give your dog the best diet possible. One with a high protein content and no grains. Raw meat is best. Some low grade kibbles can be the cause of behavioural problems, itching flaky coat, or even coprophagia (eating poo), as they desperately try and get the nutrients that they are missing in their diet
- If your dog is behaving in a way you don't like, ask yourself "what have I done to create this behaviour?" You can be sure it stems from you. Dogs in the wild have no behavioural problems
- Protect your dog, and know that he sometimes knows better than you. For example, if he is trying to take a wide berth around another dog, let him, as he is sensing bad energy. Being a good pack leader means teamwork

I am no overnight success story. I try and do a little meditation every day. Just like dog rehabilitation, it needs practice and consistency. I don't put pressure on myself to achieve this every single day, like the old me would have done, as that would make me feel bad if I didn't attain that goal, but I do it when I can. I'm much kinder to myself. And being kinder to others has followed naturally. I am definitely a more positive thinker than I used to be. My children have remarked that I am calmer than their dad these days (but he's the fun one!). I don't drink to excess any more. The memory of that hungover morning at the front door still lurks at the back of my mind and serves as a stopper.

I regularly get sent reminders from the opticians to go for a checkup, and I quietly ignore them. This only serves to remind me that I have not totally let go of the past, and have a way to go until I reach full acceptance, as fear still has its clutches over part of me. Yet I occasionally glance at the rows of spectacle cases, gathering dust, when I reach into the same drawer for my sunglasses, and I am reminded how far I have come. I am a work in progress.

I practise thankfulness every day, which makes me feel lucky, and puts a smile on my face.

I am blessed to have a wonderful supportive family and friends, a successful career, no financial stress, and to be surrounded by so much love. I thank Shirley for giving me the inspiration and courage to write my story down, create my behaviourist's website (www.bemoredog.guru) and for uttering the words 'Be More Dog'.

I continue to endeavour to see the world through a dog's eyes for my on-going peace of mind and happiness, and encourage you to do the same: to accept the things we cannot change, to play without needing to win, to show not hide our feelings, to not judge someone by their age, race or looks, to learn the art of doing nothing at all, to be less critical, to be more spontaneous, to be more open minded, to be more forgiving.

In short, to be more dog, and know that every day is the best day.